VISIONS

AND

REVISIONS

Books by Dale Peck

Greenville
Body Surfing

Gospel Harmonies
Martin and John
The Law of Enclosures
Now It's Time to Say Goodbye
The Garden of Lost and Found

Nonfiction
Hatchet Jobs
Visions and Revisions

Children's and Young Adult Fiction
Drift House
The Lost Cities
Sprout

VISIONS

AND

REVISIONS

COMING OF AGE IN THE AGE OF AIDS

DALE PECK

Portions of this book previously appeared in *Conjunctions,*
Harper's, *New York*, *Out*, *OutWeek*, *Slate*, *Swing*, and
The Village Voice Literary Supplement, as well as the anthologies
The Question of Equality and *Vital Signs.*

Published by Soho Press, Inc.
853 Broadway
New York, NY 10003

Library of Congress Cataloging-in-Publication Data

Peck, Dale.
Visions and revisions / Dale Peck.
HC ISBN 978-1-61695-441-3
PB ISBN 978-1-61695-644-8
eISBN 978-1-61695-442-0

1. Peck, Dale. 2. Authors, American—20th century—Biography.
3. Gay authors—United States—Biography. 4. AIDS activists—United
States—Biography. 5. AIDS (Disease)—Patients—Medical care—United
States. 6. AIDS (Disease)—Treatment—United States. 7. Gays—Crimes
against—United States. 8. AIDS (Disease) in literature.
9. Gays in literature. I. Title.
PS3566.E245Z46 2015
813'.54—dc 3
[B] 2014030846

Interior design by Janine Agro, Soho Press, Inc.

Printed in the United States of America

10 9 8 7 6 5 4 3 2 1

It is customary for novels, plays, essays, and pretty much anything else written about gay life in the eighties and nineties to be dedicated in memoriam to individuals—sometimes one or two, sometimes dozens or hundreds—whose lives were prematurely cut short by AIDS. Without forgetting the millions of the epidemic's dead, I would nevertheless like to break with tradition and dedicate this book, with gratitude and great respect, to Larry Kramer, because of whose tireless efforts many more millions are alive today. Including him.

And for Lou Peralta
This is the path that led me to you.

As hordes of parents hit the retail trail Friday in search of Christmas gifts for their loved ones, some may have felt a little lost among the mountains of merchandise.

What do the kids really want?

Not to fear.

—*The Hutchinson News*, Saturday, Nov. 26, 1994

1

VISIONS AND REVISIONS

grew tired and my dick grew restless. Jean-Claude and I made it through all four seasons of the year, starting in spring and ending in winter. He broke up with me during my lunch break—oh, the drama!—but we got back together, and then I broke up with him on Thanksgiving day. He came over covered in fake blood from an ACT UP demo, showered, and then we sat on Tasha's bed, he naked, I clothed, and ended it to the sounds of side two of *Who's Afraid of the Art of Noise?*, which scratched melancholically from Tasha's old record player. Later we went to Bruce and Roger's for turkey and Jean-Claude left in the middle of the meal, in tears; Bruce never forgave me for that. Damien was one of those shaved-head ACT UP clones who look simultaneously like a neo-Nazi and an inmate at Auschwitz; he told me he'd had sex with Terence Trent D'Arby in the Ramble, and that he, Terence Trent, had an *enormous* cock. Derek and I fucked almost every night for two weeks and then he went to Amsterdam; a few weeks later I was at David's apartment having my hair dyed pink when Derek showed up: David's mohawk was blue and Derek's was green, and his roots didn't need a touch-up. Dan lived with Charles and was having an affair with John; I was number three on that chain until Dan couldn't take it anymore, and one by one broke it off with all of us. Dennis was the fourth *D* in four months: he lived opposite the Hells Angels clubhouse on East 3rd Street, and the lamp on his night table was shaded with X-rays of his skull. Then Eric: after two months during which we both gained weight, he took me to Film Forum to see *Sunset Boulevard* for my twenty-fourth birthday, and then, over gelato at Raffetto's, he said, Well, Dale, it looks like our friendship is becoming a friendship. Patrick's the only one I regret, but Tasha insisted we looked good together: his skin was so coated in freckles it was orange, like his hair, and orange has always looked good on me. Eventually I took him to the Bar to break up because I didn't want to have sex first, went home that night with Frank, who'd also broken up with someone earlier in the day. John turned out to be the oldest (although François never told me his age); he had hair everywhere except his head. Barry was a palliative care nurse from Australia who just happened to be the first person to test positive Down Under—he'd helped design the nation's pilot program. Scott was British, here on an internship, and when I made out with him on the subway he flipped. A fan of cottaging, he'd had sex in public restrooms and parks and at least one cemetery, but he'd never held hands with another man on the street, let alone kissed someone on a train. Will couldn't eat food if it was served on a blue plate. That wasn't why we broke up but it was still, you know, weird. A month later I went to England to promote *Martin and John*; met Robbie; ended up spending two out of the next three years in London. When I finally gave up and moved back to New York I had the sense that there was less of me than there'd been before. I was, what? twenty-seven? twenty-eight? If you'd told me it would be another decade until I'd meet the man I was going to marry, I'd've probably slit my wrists.

marketing campaigns from alcohol manufacturers to prove it. But sex was all that remained of what we'd had before. What we'd *been* before. Sex, a few books and even fewer plays, some pictures and paintings, a handful of movies; and as a consequence every back-room blowjob, every hookup, every flushed condom and sticky-dicked walk of shame was a refusal to renounce the behavior that formed the core of our personal as well as cultural identities.

Still, for my first two or three years in the city, I obsessed over the status of ex-boyfriends and tricks, took an anxiety-ridden, morbid, but very real comfort in the fact that no one I'd slept with had died yet. *Yet*: though I never acknowledged it, a tiny voice at the back of my head was always asking: *Who will be first?* But once that question was answered, and once it happened again—and again and again—a more terrifying prospect raised its head:

Who will be last?

2

In his seminal 1987 essay "Is the Rectum a Grave?" Leo Bersani wrote, "I have been trying to account for the murderous representations of homosexuals unleashed and 'legitimized' by AIDS, and in so doing I have been struck by what might be called the aversion-displacements characteristic of both those representations and the gay responses to them." "Is the Rectum a Grave?" exposed and exploded those "murderous representations," but "the gay responses" clearly held more fascination for Bersani—specifically, the way theorists tended toward hagiography in their descriptions of pre-AIDS A-list gay culture. "We have been telling a few lies," Bersani declared, "lies whose strategic value I fully understand, but which the AIDS crisis has rendered obsolescent."

Queer theorists, Bersani argued, maintain a false position when they idealize homosexual desire, and went on to declare "particularly disheartening" the "participation of the powerless" in "finding new ways to defend our culture's lies about sexuality." Such statements placed Bersani both in- and outside the circle of his contemporaries: inside in that he opposed heterosexual bourgeois norms in the revolutionary terms then in vogue; but outside in his insistence that "to want sex with another man is not exactly a credential for political radicalism." But in its attempt to explain what, exactly, the desire for sex with another man *was* a credential for, "Is the Rectum a Grave?" proffered the seeds of its own radicalism. Phrases that described sex as "anticommunal, antiegalitarian, antinurturing, antiloving" were neither accidental nor finite. But where was Bersani going when he claimed that homosexual desire possessed a "revolutionary inaptitude" for heterosexual society, or that "Far from welcoming the return to monogamy as a beneficent consequence of the horror of AIDS, gay men should ceaselessly lament the practical necessity, now, of such relationships"?

Such provocations had to wait nearly a decade before they were picked up in his 1995 book, *Homos*, but in the interim readers were left with much to ponder, both from Bersani's essay, as well as the spate of queer theoretical projects that began appearing in the late eighties—for example, *Policing Desire* by Simon Watney, a far-reaching analysis of images of AIDS and homosexuality in the media, a review of which engendered Bersani's "Is the Rectum a Grave?", which in turn appeared in a Douglas Crimp–edited issue of *October* magazine, later reprinted in book form as *AIDS: Cultural Analysis/Cultural Activism*. Far more than a curatorial project, Crimp's anthology united a farflung group of artists, activists, and academics, and in the process created a movement, or at least revealed the movement's existence to its members, which is just as important. AIDS had blindsided the gay community in 1981. For the first several years it was all people could do to stare, and mourn, and die. But eventually grief moved beyond sorrow to anger, and in the second half of the decade we began to fight back. Eighty-seven was the key year—the year ACT UP was born, the year Crimp's issue of *October* appeared—and neither would have been what it was without the other. The particularly dense jargon favored by cultural critics, which often read as though translated from the French with a Quebecer's hostility to English, would have lacked urgency without its link to ACT UP's realpolitik, while ACT UP would have been just another group of headline-clambering discontents, morally justified but intellectually bankrupt,

Feuerbach could have been our mantra during what my friend the playwright Gordon Armstrong called "our era of crisis" (the key word here: not "crisis" but "our"), when personal tragedy and political triumph swirled together like oil in water. Indeed, it was like an oil spill: some days gripped you in paralyzing sludge, other days a single spark threatened to blow everything away. But every time you felt ready to give up someone would come along with another idea, another strategy, another chant. Virginia Apuzzo, Allan Bérubé, Kate Bornstein, John Boswell, Michael Bronski, Judith Butler, Pat Califia, Michael Callen, George Chauncey, Andrea Dworkin, Lillian Faderman, Leslie Feinberg, David Halperin, Larry Kramer, Audre Lorde, Cindy Patton, Vito Russo, Sarah Schulman, Eve Kosofsky Sedgwick, Urvashi Vaid, Michael Warner, Jeffrey Weeks, Monique Wittig, David Wojnarowicz. The people queers looked to for inspiration then, the people they called their leaders, were known for their accomplishments—their *ideas*—and didn't simply parlay celebrity into a (pseudo-) political platform. As befit the times, the agenda wasn't assimilationist but interventionist. People didn't argue for marriage equality, they argued against the bureaucratization and commodification of love (even a neocon like Allan Bloom got that one right), while the concept of gays in the military was about as welcome at an ACT UP or Queer Nation meeting as ROTC recruiters at Columbia University during the Vietnam War. And despite Susan Sontag's pointed reminder in *AIDS and Its Metaphors* against the danger of war analogies as again—"the revelatory aspect of our time." I remember Bob Rafsky delivering a eulogy off the top of his head at the same memorial service, and I remember being filled with hope because here was a man creating political oratory that seemed to me as epochal as any homily by Daniel Webster or Henry Ward Beecher that I studied in college. And I remember looking at Mark Fisher's face beneath the clear top of his coffin, and it was at that moment I lost hope. At the time of Fisher's death I had been more or less absent from ACT UP for several months, primarily to prepare my first novel for publication, but also because I was having misgivings about ACT UP's continued efficacy, especially in the wake of the decision of key members of the Treatment and Data Committee—the so-called "science guys"—to splinter off into a new and pointedly independent organization called the Treatment Action Group. During the course of its first five years ACT UP had perfected a strategy that paired epistemology with epidemiology, creating spectacles of political theater that were perfectly positioned to the media age and given moral weight by irrefutable scientific and bureaucratic fact. But by 1992 the media had become savvy to ACT UP's tactics, or perhaps just bored of them, and, in the wake of TAG's departure, statements that had formerly been pitched to a specific research or political agenda devolved into misdirection, drawing the audience's attention not to the AIDS epidemic but to AIDS activists themselves. Trying to refocus the story on the ever-widening sphere of the

epidemic—on the need, say, for needle-exchange pro-
grams to prevent the spread of HIV among injection-drug
users, or studies investigating how the virus and its
medications worked in women's bodies as opposed to
men's—was like trying to teach a cat to fetch: no matter
how wildly you gesticulated toward the object of attention,
the stupid, obstinate, or perhaps simply perverse pupil
would look only at your pointing finger.

But a few weeks before Mark Fisher's memorial service
I rejoined ACT UP. I had marched in the memorial proces-
sion for David Wojnarowicz on July 29, 1992, and I had been
present at the Ashes Action on October 11, 1992, when the
cremated remains of people who had died of AIDS were
thrown over the fence that surrounded the Bush White
House, but this, it seemed to me, was a totem of a different
order. In fact it wasn't a totem at all: it was a *body*, and I had
come back to ACT UP to walk with it through the streets of
New York City because I thought the statement Mark Fisher
had chosen to make with his life and with his death and
with his corpse was so powerful that America—that Americans, if not America's leaders—could not ignore it. But they
had. New Yorkers, who love a spectacle more than anyone
else, had looked at Mark Fisher's face and then their own
faces had hardened and they had looked away; and as I
looked at Mark Fisher's face I knew that despite five years
of ACT UP—despite the Wall Street action in 1987 and the
St. Patrick's demo in 1989 and the Day of Desperation in
1991, despite the front-page press coverage that had

attended these spectacles and the hundreds of thousands of dollars raised through the sale of T-shirts and posters and stickers and pins, despite Rock Hudson and Ryan White and Magic Johnson, despite Elizabeth Glaser's speech at the Democratic National Convention on July 14, 1992 and Mary Fisher's speech at the Republican National Convention on August 19, 1992, despite 200,000 deaths in the United States and twelve million people infected worldwide—despite *fifteen years of plague* New Yorkers still looked at people with AIDS in the same way they looked at Mark Fisher: through a sheet of glass. Through a screen. AIDS wasn't their problem, but the problem of people who lived and died somewhere else and only entered their consciousness through their televisions, at which point they hurriedly changed the channel. I myself hadn't known Mark Fisher except by sight. I don't know that I ever spoke to him. But I had walked with his dead body up Sixth Avenue at rush hour for more than fifty blocks and watched thousands of people look at his face through the clear top of his coffin, and those people *had not cared*. And if they hadn't cared about this body, then why should they care about the words said over it? Why should they care what those words meant? It seemed to me that those words lacked even smoke's ephemeral substance before it disappears: even as they were spoken, they were no longer there. Twenty-one years later, I don't remember a thing anyone said. I remember only the act of speaking, and Mark Fisher's body.

3

Thomas Mulcahy died a few months before Mark Fisher, in July of 1992. At the time of his death he'd been a fifty-seven-year-old sales executive for a company called Bull HN Information Systems living in Sudbury, Massachusetts, a "comfortable suburb," according to the *New York Times*, "fifteen miles west of Boston." He had worked at one time in South Africa; had fathered four children; was married to a woman named Margaret; and, again according to the *Times*, gardened "busily" and to great praise from his neighbors. He was described by the *Times*, twice, as "active in his church," and his cousin, a Catholic priest, said mass at his funeral. One can assume from his last name that Mulcahy had been Irish, although this detail, and pretty much everything else mentioned in the *Times*, was over-shadowed by the shocking nature of his death, and by a single other fact: Thomas Mulcahy was a closet case. Though ostensibly in New York City to give a sales presentation on July 8, 1992, he went first, on July 7, to the Townhouse, a restaurant on the Upper East Side with a reputation as a hustler bar, and from there, at 11:30 P.M., to an auto-mated teller machine, and then, rather than return to his room at the Barbizon Hotel, he went at some unknown time with the person or persons who eventually dumped seven plastic garbage bags containing pieces of his body, and an eighth that contained his briefcase, along two highways in Ocean County, New Jersey.

Mulcahy might have continued to rest in whatever kind of peace a man who's been hacked to pieces can rest in if the body of Anthony Marrero hadn't turned up ten months later, in May 1993. Like Mulcahy, Marrero was found in garbage bags—this time six—that were scattered along a highway in Ocean County, and like Mulcahy simplistic generalizations can be made about his life based on information that was widely reported: Anthony Marrero was a crack addict. Anthony Marrero was a Port Authority hustler, which is to say that Anthony Marrero earned $10, as opposed to $150, to do in a public restroom what higher-priced hustlers—the kind of hustlers who were said to frequent the Townhouse—do in apartments and expensive hotels, and Anthony Marrero was gay, or perhaps bisexual, though in either case he didn't deal with it very well. He had been married once, divorced, and according to his brother continued to "see" women. He had been born in Puerto Rico in 1949, raised in Philadelphia, and spent five years on the road after his marriage ended, landing in New York in 1985. But what made Marrero of interest to readers of New York newspapers was not, as the *Times* told us, that he once tried out as a pitcher for the Phillies, but that he was the second of three victims of a serial killer whose m.o. was distinguished by two things: he picked up gay men, and when he was done with them he chopped them into pieces.

Michael Sakara was the third victim. Parts of his body were never found, but the parts that were recovered turned up in Rockland County in Upstate New York. His head and arms, as the *Times, Post,* and *Washington Blade* all pointed out, were happened upon by a hot-dog vendor in Haverstraw on July 31, 1993, though only *Newsday* reported that they were dropped at a "scenic overlook"; the scene that was overlooked wasn't reported. His torso was found by a volunteer firefighter on August 1 in Stony Point, more than twenty-five miles away. Other facts: Michael Sakara was fifty-six years old at the time of his death. He was six feet four inches tall and weighed 250 pounds. Until January 1993 his lover of nine years had lived with him in a studio at 771 West End Avenue, and until July 29 of that year, or the 30th, or the 31st, he had been employed by the *New York Law Journal* as a typesetter, where he reported in at 2:15 P.M. For more than twenty years he went to the Five Oaks piano bar almost every night, and when, in the mid-eighties, he began singing at the piano, "he ended each night," according to the *Times*, "with a vamp of 'I'll Be Seeing You.'"

Twenty-one years later, this piece of information still strikes me as a quintessential example of what Joan Didion called, in *The White Album*, "the kind of 'ironic' detail the reporters would seize upon, the morning the bodies were found," and like Didion I find myself alienated rather than moved by such tone-deaf accounting. "I'll Be Seeing You," the Phillies tryout, the fact that Thomas Mulcahy lived among the sort of people who complimented him on the number of annuals he planted. Did New Yorkers really need to know, as Mike McAlary informed *Newsday* readers, that

Michael Sakara "used to joke that he wouldn't be caught dead in an automobile"? Writers of these anecdotes labor under two misperceptions: the first is that, unless readers know something about a victim, they won't understand the tragedy of murder, and the second is that a four-paragraph capsule biography can possibly carry the weight of a human life. (In fact readers never understand the tragedy of murder, and the biography has yet to be written that conveys the burden of a body as you walk with it up a city street.) And of course these summaries tend toward the homogenizing as well: the gay facts, the dirty facts as it were, of Thomas Mulcahy and Anthony Marrero and Michael Sakara's lives are presented, but it is the sanitary details of the flower garden and the Phillies tryout that are emphasized, "the old familiar places" that are invested with the emotional tug of anecdote, all of which is done in an effort to make Thomas Mulcahy and Anthony Marrero and Michael Sakara, who may or may not have had anything in common with you or me, seem just like "you and me." Because in this notion of shared humanity, "you and me" are not crack addicts or alcoholics and "you and me" are not prostitutes. "We" do not step out on our wives or girlfriends to pick up men for sex in restaurants and bars and bus stations because "we" are not closet cases because "we," most important, are not gay.

SO WE WERE being killed in the summer of 1993. This, too, is a simplification, and probably melodramatic as well.

Nevertheless most queers know we are being killed every summer, in ones and twos, in fives and tens and twenties. The summer of 1993, however, the killings were brutal enough and numerous enough, the details of the cases sensational enough, that for two weeks the story of gay death was considered "newsworthy," which is another way of saying that it was "of general interest," which meant, in short, that straight people could be assumed to want to read about gay death. At any rate it was more interesting than yet another closeted actor dying of AIDS.

And, as well, it seemed that not only were we being killed in the summer of 1993, but that murder was following me around. A few months earlier, in fact, in February, I had traveled to Milwaukee to write about Jeffrey Dahmer on the occasion of the first anniversary of his conviction of the murder of sixteen men. A year and a half before that, when the case broke in July of '91, I had been in San Francisco, on what turned out to be a fucking vacation. I spent four of six nights—maybe it was five of seven—tricking with someone, but because I didn't keep a datebook then, I don't remember exactly when I started reading about the serial murderer who preyed on Milwaukee's gay black men. But I think it was on the morning of my first full day there, so that Jeffrey Lionel Dahmer became as much a part of my trip as did Anthony, and Matt, and later Anthony and his boyfriend Sammy. At the time I didn't obsessively record the names of my tricks as I would later, and so I've forgotten the names of one, or maybe two, of the men I had sex with. Jeffrey Dahmer, I read, also forgot the names of his men. What he remembered was their bodies, and what he did to them. What I remember is mornings at the Café Flore, a cappuccino, the *San Francisco Chronicle*—and Jeffrey Dahmer. Milwaukee seemed far from America's gay mecca, but Jeffrey Dahmer seemed quite close, not so much in the mornings when I was reading about him as in the evenings, in some bar or sex club or apartment, when the question would inevitably come up: *Would you have gone home with him?* It was a question I asked myself again in February 1993 when I visited the derelict industrial block of South 2nd Street in Milwaukee that was home to the city's tiny strip of gay bars, otherwise known as Dahmer's "hunting grounds." The 219 came first. Neon tubes poked from the three floors above the bar, glowing pink and blue like the tubes on the outside of Mars once did, back in the days when New York's Meatpacking District was still mostly meatpackers and gay clubs. Inside there was even more neon than outside, too many airbrushed photographs of naked men, a sparse crowd of ten or fifteen, all white—a change from Dahmer's day, I was told, when the bar's clientele was mostly black. The C'est La Vie was next, a carbon copy of the 219, and then the last bar on the strip: the Phoenix. The local hustler bar. From the entrance you could see—and be seen by—virtually the entire room, a deep featureless rectangle like a nail salon in a strip mall, although the dim, damp, smoky air made it feel as claustrophobic as a refrigerator box tipped over on its side. Three white drag queens stared at the door, waiting. In their anyone where he was going because there was no one to tell, and for a few dollars more he would meekly hold out his thin wrists to be handcuffed for the "bondage" photo. He would drink a drugged drink. He would never wake up. And he would never be missed.

Flash forward four months: June 1993, London, where I had made arrangements to stay the summer with my friend Scott, who'd returned to England after his internship ended the year before. I'd been in the country for less than three hours when I was awakened by a phone call from a reporter for the *Sunday Times*, who tracked me down through my agent in New York to ask me what, exactly, gay men who "practice sadomasochism" do in bed that leaves them vulnerable to murder. It was several minutes before the reporter could make my jet-lagged brain understand that the bodies of five London men had been discovered over the course of the previous four months, and that all five had been tied up and strangled in their homes. Four of the men, she told me, were openly gay, at least to friends, and three were believed to "practice sadomasochism" and were probably picked up in leather bars. I, as a gay writer whose work seemed, in the opinion of the reporter who called me, to have something to do with sadomasochism, had been singled out, tracked down, and woken up to comment on the lives of these five men I knew nothing about.

Later I learned a few things. I learned that Peter Walker was forty-five when he died. Christopher Dunn was thirty-seven. Perry Bradley was thirty-five. Andrew Collier was thirty-three, Emanuel Spiteri forty-one. I learned that Peter Walker was the assistant director of the West End production of *City of Angels*. Christopher Dunn was a children's librarian at Harlesden Library. Perry Bradley, an American, was international sales director at J-B Weld, an adhesives manufacturer, Andrew Collier took care of the old people who lived at Greenacre Court in Hackney, and Emanuel Spiteri, born in Malta, worked as a catering assistant at Imperial College in Kensington. I learned that Peter Walker was found on March 10, 1993, Christopher Dunn on May 30, 1993, Perry Bradley and Andrew Collier on June 7, 1993, and June 9, 1993, respectively, and Emanuel Spiteri on June 15, 1993, the day I arrived in London. I learned, in other words, only what I read in the papers, which is to say, only what the papers found worth telling. What I didn't learn was how these men lived, nor even, excluding the obvious mechanical facts, how they died.

For most Londoners—for straight Londoners anyway, and for gay Londoners who didn't "practice sadomasochism" or considered themselves prettier than the killer's middle-aged, overweight victims—the case was essentially a six-week-long media blitz. (From my journal of June 23, 1993: "They've released a description of the serial killer: white, between 30–40, large build (fat or muscle no one said; clearly, not fags working this case), short hair (I think) & clean-shaven as of 2 weeks ago. Oh, and he has 'discoloured teeth.' Well, I suspect I won't be asking him home anytime soon.") It wasn't until a few days after the fourth victim, Andrew Collier, was found on June 9 that the public was made aware of the serial killings, and by July 30 an unemployed thirty-nine-year-old named Colin Ireland had been arrested and charged in two of the murders; he was later charged in, and pleaded guilty to, all five. But before the arrest London had first, depending on one's point of view, to be amused by or suffer through the reporting of the murders, and my eight weeks in England were punctuated by the press accounts of the story much as my time in San Francisco had been marked by the Dahmer spectacle. Only this time the story was more intimate—more titillating—because I was in the same city as the killer, and the killer was, at least initially, still at large. There was, in the first week, the requisite soft-pedaling of the victims' lives. The *Daily Star* summed up Emanuel Spiteri this way: "One former barman—nicknamed 'Cinders'—said: 'He was always cheerful, with a nice personality and a pretty face.'" (One imagines Mary outside her son's tomb: "He had such a lovely disposition. Didn't complain even when they drove the nails in.") There was, shortly afterward, the "investigative" journalism into London's gay BDSM scene. One bar, the Coleherne, was referred to as the "Coal Urn" (c.f. Cinders?) when a reporter relied on the pronunciation rather than the spelling skills of his interviewee. I found signs when I went to another bar, the Block, posted in the corner where sex, when it happened, happened, informing a crowd of men whose activities didn't seem much affected that, because of the serial killer, "reporters might be present." There was, still in the opening weeks, the expected AIDS hysteria: three of the victims, it turned out, were HIV-positive, and for a few weeks an "AIDS-revenge" motive was bandied about; this wasn't abandoned, exactly, but the complete lack of proof made it hard to discuss without appearing to speculate. Then there were reports of a series of phone calls made by the killer to the Metropolitan Police, press, and other groups. Thus the killer's lack of respect for gay life was matched, we learned from the *Daily Mail*, only by his concern for dogs: after killing Peter Walker he called up the Samaritans to rescue the animals trapped in their murdered master's flat. Early in July there was the "videofit," a computer-generated image based on witnesses' descriptions of a man who was assumed to be the killer, and there was, a week later, the fuzzy still from a video camera mounted in a tube station showing, clearly, Emanuel Spiteri and, obliquely, a tall, fattish man following him. A week later a nearly identical still, referred to as the "enhanced" image, was released; the only additional details I could make out were the fat man's shoe and part of his shoulder. Toward the end of July there was the tabloids' long-sought-after visit with Dennis Nilsen, convicted in 1983 of murdering six gay men, and suspected in the deaths of nine more. Cast by both the press and himself in the role of Hannibal Lecter, Nilsen wrote in a letter printed in the *Evening Standard*, "Hate is not a factor in this maladaptive conundrum"; rather, he told readers, "the multifarious circumstances of [the killer's] life came to a converging crisis in March and triggered him on his one-way ticket to multiple homicide." There was, finally, the arrest, but by this time the multifarious circumstances of this maladaptive conundrum—dead queers, kinky sex practices, taunting phone calls, and psychokiller psycho-babble—had come to their converging crisis, and were now used up. Reports of the arrest, where it was reported, were limited to the back pages, and then, in my final two weeks in London, there was nothing at all.

The media that reported this story were London's tab-loids—the *Sun*, the *Mirror*, the *Star*, the *Mail*—and they laid it out with their usual combination of tact, compassion, and nuance. The story figured in the gay press, of course, in the *Pink Paper* and *Capital Gay* and *Gay Times*, was given its due in the mainstream dailies, the conservative *Times*, *Tele-graph*, and *Evening Standard*, the more liberal *Independent* and *Guardian*. But it was the *News of the World* that found it necessary to run photographs from a gay BDSM catalog beside photographs of the victims, and it was the *Sun* that felt the need to explain—incorrectly, as it turned out—the rudiments of the handkerchief code, and, as they say, it would have been funny if it hadn't been grotesque. Now, it should be noted that by 1993 London had a chapter of ACT UP. London had a Queer Nation. London had a group of its own creation, OutRage!, and London had Boy George and Jimmy Somerville and Sir Ian McKellen. London even had Simon Watney, author of *Policing Desire,* the urtext of queer media criticism. But in a city where it was *illegal for same-sex couples to hold hands or kiss in public*, it seems safe to say that London's queers didn't wield even the qualified political power that New York's did. It was a group called Gay London Policing that first suggested to the Metropolitan Police that the murders might be the work of one person, and later served as a conduit for information from gay witnesses reluctant to speak directly to the police. But GALOP aside, ACT UP and Queer Nation and OutRage! aside, London's queers couldn't do anything about the homophobic sentiments that appeared in the press for six weeks. Just one example: "The gay scene is ideal for killing," the *Daily Express* quoted a forensic psychologist as saying. "If the killer is good-looking, and regarded as something of a catch, then his victims might not be asking too many questions." It occurred to me as I read that line that it was exactly what the reporter from the *Sunday Times* was hoping I would say to her.

WHEN, IN AUGUST, I left London, and Colin Ireland, and Peter Walker and Christopher Dunn and Perry Bradley and Andrew Collier and Emanuel Spiteri and the *Sun* and the *Mirror* and the *Daily Express*, I arrived back in New York to read in the *Times* and *Newsday* and the *Post* and the *Daily News* about Michael Sakara and Anthony Marrero and Thomas Mulcahy, and, shortly afterward, an editor from the *Village Voice* contacted me and asked me to write my own version of this story—a kind of *Tale of Two Cities*, only this time the cities would be London and New York and the war would be against homosexuals rather than the *ancien régime*. It was only the second reported story of my career and already the second about gay serial killers. In truth the story should have been old news by the time I returned to New York, had the New York City Police Department and, by extension, the press chosen to take note of it after Anthony Marrero had been murdered three months earlier, in May. The NYPD had been made aware of the murder of Thomas Mulcahy in July 1992 by both New Jersey police and the New York City Gay and Lesbian Anti-Violence Project, because the last place Thomas Mulcahy had been seen alive was the Townhouse, on the Upper East Side of Manhattan. The NYPD had again been contacted by Jersey police and AVP after the murder of Anthony Marrero in May 1993, and, further, had been made aware that both New Jersey cops and AVP were, according to Bea Hanson, AVP's Director of Client Services, "making connections between [Marrero] and the Mulcahy body." Both times the NYPD declined to get involved because, according to Hanson, "the bodies were found outside of New York state . . . even though the origination of the crimes was in New York City." Instead, the NYPD adopted a wait-and-see attitude, which meant, essentially, that it would wait to investigate and it would wait to inform New York's gay community of the possibility of a serial killer until another gay man was killed. In the meantime, according to Hanson, "New Jersey cops came [into New York City] and we worked with them to check out bars. New York City cops could have easily done that."

another killer or killers.* What Mayor Dinkins's speech left New Yorkers with, then, were three dead gay men (Mulcahy, Marrero, Sakara) murdered by one person, and a fourth dead gay man (Anderson) who, as it turned out, was murdered by the same person, although at the time it looked like he'd been murdered by some other person or persons. But by bringing Peter Anderson into the discussion, Dinkins had, wittingly or unwittingly, brought in Julio Prado, who had been murdered January 11, 1992, Van Pleasant, murdered July 19, 1992, Roosevelt Lewis, murdered March 3, 1993, Lawrence Andrews, March 1993, Dwight Greene, July 1993, and Jimmy Hawkins, who had been found in his apartment on August 15, 1993 with his throat slashed and thirty-one additional stab wounds puncturing his body. All of these men—like, presumably, Peter Anderson and Thomas Mulcahy and Anthony Marrero and Michael Sakara—had been murdered by men they picked up for a night of sex.

"This is all happening," Bea Hanson told me, "in the context of another group of murders that the police have virtually ignored. In most of these other cases the police

---

*On May 27, 2001, after the development of a technique called vacuum metal deposition made it possible to recover fingerprints from plastic, Richard W. Rogers, a fifty-one-year-old Staten Island resident, was arrested for, and later convicted of, the murders of Anthony Marrero and Thomas Mulcahy. He remains the sole suspect in the murders of Michael Sakara, Peter Anderson, and Matthew John Pierro, whose body was recovered in Lake Mary, Florida, on April 10, 1982, with a bite mark that was said by an odontologist to have been made by Rogers; Rogers's fingerprints—which were on file because he had killed "an acquaintance" in 1973, for which he was acquitted on grounds of self-defense—were found at the crime scene. The murder of Guillermo Mendez (who wasn't gay) remains unsolved.

have not made an effort to work with the gay community." It was, perhaps, a rhetorical question, but I asked it anyway: did Hanson think homophobia was a factor in the police department's decision not to investigate these cases? "It's absolutely homophobia. Even in the pick-up cases that aren't murder cases the majority of the police response is, 'Well, why'd you bring the guy home anyway?' Then you have a murder: 'So it's a couple of fags dead. Big deal.'" Hanson continued: "There is, I think, a sort of homophobia that goes on that gives the police an excuse to not really investigate. Investigating means connecting with the gay and lesbian community. It means going to gay bars, so that officers need to keep confronting their own homophobia over and over again. And in addition to the homophobia that's shrouding this whole investigation is the dimension of racism. Anthony Marrero, who was a Latino man [and] a street hustler, hasn't gotten the kind of attention that someone like Thomas Mulcahy received. In the Mulcahy case, after his body was found, they assigned a detective to work specifically on that case. Anthony Marrero didn't get any detective assigned to him."

"It's a shame that we have to wait until there is a bona fide string of these incidents before we can get any attention," Matt Foreman, AVP's executive director, told the *Post*, although it appeared that what it actually took to get police or press attention was not just "a bona fide string of these incidents," but a bona fide string of incidents attributable to just one person. "We have been trying to get the police department to respond to this since July of last year," Bea Hanson told the *Washington*

Blade. "This could have been stopped earlier." Hanson's words sounded familiar to me. The same thing had been said in Milwaukee, of course, by both its gay and its black citizens. But that wasn't what I was thinking of. Ten years earlier, in the March 14–27, 1983 issue of the *New York Native*, in an essay entitled "1,112 and Counting," Larry Kramer had written: "We desperately need something from our government to save our lives, and we're not getting it." Kramer's essay had come some twenty months after the *New York Times*'s "Rare Cancer Seen in 41 Homosexuals" headline of July 3, 1981, and, just as the *Times* article is generally regarded as the first news story about AIDS, Kramer's piece is generally regarded as the first essay about AIDS, though both of these details are less important than the fact that Kramer had gone on to make the same demands for the next decade, and the *Times* had not. But despite the fact that 1,112 had jumped to 360,909—and counting—we still weren't getting what we needed from our government.

And yes, I know: that's probably melodramatic too. But it doesn't make it any less true.

4

April 19, 1991

I'm getting ready to take a disco nap when Suki, Tasha's cat, starts to whine. I look at the clock: almost 6:30. She's not fed till seven. I've gone out the past several Fridays (and most Saturdays, and a few Sundays) and the truth is I'm a little bored with the scene, though some new developments have made it more interesting. And I haven't hung out in a while with CB, who's driving in from Connecticut, so that'll be nice. But it's been a long day capping a long week, and I'm not going to do anything if I don't get some sleep—and Suki, who can scream like she's dying of feline leukemia, isn't about to let that happen. "You win," I tell her, coming out of my room. I dump some Science Diet for mature cats in her bowl, then head back to my futon.

CB buzzes at nine. "I'll wait for you in the car," he tells the intercom. CB has this thing about cars: his last one was stolen (while he was having dinner with me, as it happens), and this one's been broken into three times in six months, so maybe it's justified.

Downstairs, I notice the absence of his current beau. "Where's Jay?" I ask. "Jay's at home," CB tells me.

I met Jay at a birthday party a week ago. I'd heard about him for weeks—how he'd grown up on a ranch in Montana, how he met CB the first time he walked into a gay bar, how he'd been engaged to a woman who was now "back in Montana." As a phenomenon Jay fascinated me: The Young Gay Man Upon First Coming Out. Though only twenty-two, a year younger than me, at the party Jay had seemed like a teenager, hanging his head, smiling a lot (but not talking), hiding behind CB. When he thought no one was looking he'd put his hand on the back of CB's neck and let his fingers play over the skin. When I saw that, I remembered CB telling me that Jay had gone home with him without even a kiss first. I thought both actions stemmed from Jay's nervousness about being gay ("Well actually," he told me at the birthday party, "I don't like to label myself."), but then I remembered something else CB had said. At his house CB had tried to kiss Jay, and Jay had pushed him away. "How do you get AIDS?" he'd demanded. So instead of sex that first night, they'd had sex ed.

"Jay told me the other night that he's definitely gay," CB tells me as we drink Rolling Rocks and drive through the park. "But I don't think he's ready for this." No, I have to agree, he's probably not.

In 1984 HIV was identified as the cause of AIDS, but despite this fact, and the concomitant discovery that transmission of the virus could be prevented through fairly simple modifications to sexual activity—i.e., safe sex—in 1985 Ed Koch closed New York City's bathhouses, sex clubs, and back rooms (heterosexual as well as homosexual, to be fair to Hizzoner) in the name of preventing the spread of HIV, and for the past six years public sex has been pretty much absent from New York. But David Dinkins defeated Koch in the 1989 Democratic primary, then defeated Rudy Giuliani in the 1989 general election, and almost as soon as he took office in 1990 things began to relax. Now Limelight, a Catholic church turned nightclub, has decided to test the waters by opening a back room at Mea Culpa, its Friday night party. The sex room is located in what used to be the friary, so people aren't doing anything there that hasn't been done before, except perhaps dancing.

As a college student in New Jersey I'd read Guy Trebay's account in the *Village Voice* of the last days of the Mineshaft. I'd read Edmund White's description of alfresco sex on the West Side piers in *Nocturnes for the King of Naples* and Andrew Holleran's tales of hedonism in the Everard Baths in *Dancer From the Dance* and Larry Kramer's debauched description of same in *Faggots*. It's not that I *wanted* to visit a sex club: I felt *compelled* to. The gay identity I was adopting as both a man and a writer was epicurean, libertine, and quite possibly not good for me. In lieu of discrete acts of missionary monogamy, sex had become vertical, social, with innumerable partners coalescing and drifting apart in scenarios that could go on for hours, days even, though none of the players at the end might have been present at the beginning. And now, finally, I was getting a chance to find out what all the fuss was about.

Downstairs, some go-go boys are dancing atop the bar, and CB and I conduct a pseudointellectual discussion about the unsexiness of strippers so we can pretend our gawking is derisory rather than desirous. After a while that gets boring, so we dance. We drink. We separate. I find myself at the door of the sex room, which gapes at me like a big black mouth. The idea of anonymity is qualified as soon as I walk in and see CB. Unsure of the etiquette, I do my best to keep us in separate social circles, but, stealing a glance at his partner, I realize I know him too. I'm trying to remember if he and CB have ever met when someone puts his hand on my crotch and I forget about CB. It's not as if my mind turns off or anything. If anything, I'm cerebrating even more than I did with the go-go boys—although, to be fair to myself, I should mention that I'd agreed before the fact to write about this experience, so I was primed to give it an intellectual frisson. No, that's not quite right either. The truth is I'd heard about Mea Culpa's back room weeks before but, despite five years of fantasizing about just this sort of thing, hadn't worked up the nerve to check it out. But when an editor at *OutWeek* announced that the magazine was doing a feature on "a night in queer New York," I immediately offered to cover Limelight. So I'm not just getting my rocks off: I'm working. But I'm also, you know, getting my rocks off, in the former friary of an old church filled with twenty or thirty men.

This is so seventies, I tell myself. I tell myself that queers have freed sex from quaint notions of commitment and meaning and consequence, but as I look around at the men in this room, many of whom are in their thirties and forties, I find myself wondering if any of them still thinks that, or remembers a time before AIDS when it might have actually been true. I wonder if they feel guilty now, or lucky, or afraid—but then some hairy-chested dude with poppers-glazed eyes pinches my nipple while someone else whose face I haven't really seen applies his mouth to my cock, and for a moment the scene is reduced to its physical parameters. My body; his—and his, and his. There's a dick in each of my hands. Wait, let me rephrase that: there's a *dick* in each of my *hands*! One goes with the hairy chest, but I'm not sure what the other's connected to. I wouldn't mind doing a little sucking myself, but my lips are chapped and the bottom one might have a small cut, so no kissing for me, let alone sucking. (Jay's voice in my head: "How do you get AIDS?") I lid my eyes and try to impersonate poppers guy, who's moaning porn aphorisms: "Yeah, baby, do it." "Oh yeah, pull on that thing." The guy's hot, but the blankness of his expression is off-putting, and the words coming out of his mouth are a reminder that no experience is ever just physical. Somewhere along the line this guy learned to think of his drivel as erotic, and I find myself wondering who his performance is for: me, or himself? It's all a bit much, and I close my eyes and pretend I'm mastur-bating with somebody else's mouth. I come; I go.

On the drive home, I thank God for CB's car: my idea of sexual denouement isn't a subway ride. "How was Alex?" I ask. "Alex?" "My friend, Alex. That's the guy you ended up with." "Oh," CB says. "He came on my shirt." He shows me the spot, as innocuous as a water stain. We talk about how strange it must have been, in the days before the sex clubs were closed down, to have done this every weekend, every night even; in hindsight, I find it telling that we used the word "strange" rather than "exciting" or "addictive" or, I don't know, "enervating." CB drops me off and heads back to Connecticut, and Jay. It's morbid, but I can't help wonder-ing how many gay men went out for a night as equivocal as the one I just had and died for it. Upstairs, my roommates are sleeping and the cat has this funny idea I'm going to feed her. I don't though. I just brush my teeth and wash my hands—and then, remembering, my dick—and go to bed.

5

In the wake of later developments, it's easy to forget that back rooms, sex clubs, and bathhouses re-emerged not because of some newfound tolerance by straight people (or their elected officials) for the more risqué aspects of the gay milieu, but because even the most rudimentary under-standing of how HIV is transmitted will tell you that it's hard to get, which is one of the reasons why everyone in the world isn't infected or, well, dead. That group sex and promiscuity were significant factors in the virus's spread in the gay community in the first years of the epidemic—which is to say, before the invention of safe sex by Richard Berkowitz and Michael Callen in 1982 (or, to be more accu-rate, before their tactics were endorsed by a government reluctant to acknowledge the existence of homosexual intercourse, let alone talk about it)—is borne out by the demographics of infection in the developed world. But according to the Centers for Disease Control, the rate of new HIV infections peaked in 1983 and 1984, just as the tech-niques of safe sex began to be widely disseminated, and, by 1986, new infections had dropped by about 25% and held steady for the next four or five years—which is to say, until around the time the sex clubs began to reopen—at which point new HIV infections *dropped* another 25%. And, though most of the clubs and back rooms closed after another three or four or five years, infection rates have remained more or less steady since 1992, with approximately 50,000 Americans seroconverting each year.

A significant portion of these new infections, however—between 60% and 80% depending on the year—occur among "men who have sex with men," or MSM, as the CDC terms them. By way of explanation for this phenomenon, the CDC, in its *Estimated HIV Incidence Among Adults and Adolescents in the United States 2007–2010*, reports that

> individual risk behavior alone does not account for the disproportionate burden of HIV among young MSM. Other factors are likely at work, including: higher prevalence of HIV among MSM, which leads to a greater risk of HIV exposure with each sexual encounter; the high proportion of young MSM (especially young MSM of color) who are unaware of their infection, which increases the risk of unknowingly transmitting the virus to others; stigma and homophobia, which deter some from seeking HIV prevention services; barriers, such as lack of insurance and concerns about confidentiality, that result in less access to testing, care, and

antiretroviral treatment; and high rates of some STDs, which can facilitate HIV transmission. Additionally, many young MSM may underestimate their personal risk for HIV.

What the data and the analysis show, then, is that some gay men have persisted in having sex without condoms since the invention of safe sex, which, because of the high rate of HIV infection among gay men, makes their chances of becoming infected significantly higher than heterosexuals'. The second part of this phenomenon was, of course, well-known from the early years of the epidemic, but the first part remained something of an *in camera* conversation until the mid-nineties, when a series of articles in the gay and nongay press brought it to broader public attention. The most widely regarded of these pieces is probably Michael Warner's "Why Gay Men Are Having Risky Sex," which appeared in the January 31, 1995 issue of the *Village Voice*. Warner was already a well-known queer theorist (in *Homos*, which would come out a few months later, Leo Bersani named him a chief architect of the terminological shift from "gay" to "queer"), and he made the discussion personal by admitting he'd had an "unsafe encounter" himself. The experience left him understandably rattled, not to mention frightened for his health, and as a teacher and writer he looked to the literature to try to find out "why I wanted risky sex." But "in the vast industry of AIDS education and prevention, I knew of nothing that would help me answer this question."

Warner's confession became a touchstone for a discussion still going on today, both in terms of practical efforts to get gay men to have safe sex, and in the theoretical world as well—as late as 2007, David Halperin published *What Do Gay Men Want?*, a book-length response to some of the issues raised in Warner's then twelve-year-old essay. Warner's thesis aside—that "abjection" is attractive to certain gay men, who take "pleasure in being the lowest of the low, in being bad, in being outlaws, in betraying both our own values and those of the people around us"—his essay was a level-headed but urgent call for prevention education to move beyond paraphernalia and practice to the psychology of sex, both individual and cultural, and it stood in stark contrast to a slew of articles then appearing in New York's mainstream press. These articles didn't so much discuss the supposed reemergence of unsafe sex as decry it, although the truth is they focused less on sex than on certain of the venues in which it took place, i.e., back rooms and sex clubs, which in turn led to the formation, in early 1995, in New York City, of a group calling itself Gay and Lesbian HIV Prevention Activists. "HIV transmission among gay men is becoming epidemic again," GLHPA declared in one of its first leaflets, and the program it outlined "to end HIV transmission in commercial sex establishments" essentially called for the closure of those establishments. This was danced around: all GLHPA actually asked was that HIV educational materials be prominently displayed in "commercial sex establishments"; that these establishments provide regular educational sessions on protected sex; and that, in accordance with pre-existing health code regulations, anal or vaginal or oral intercourse not occur. Additionally, GLHPA asked that such sexual activity as was legally permissible (which seemed to be confined to hand-jobs and toesucking), must be monitorable, meaning adequate lighting and no cubicles, and, finally, that it must also be monitored—which meant, in those few "commercial sex establishments" that made a good-faith effort to demonstrate their commitment to safe sex, the shadowy presence of three or four men, usually South Asian immigrants and always heterosexual, dressed in black like stage hands and peering squeamishly over shoulders and through legs in an attempt to determine whether a too-eager pole was trying to gain entry to an unguarded hole like some misguided bridge-and-tunneler trying to slip past the doorman at Studio 54. I remember trying to imagine how one might derive erotic satisfaction in an environment that sounded more like an examining room than a sex club, but all I could come up with was a riddle I learned as a kid: if there are seventeen birds sitting on a branch and you manage to hit three of them with a single shotgun blast, how many will remain on the tree? Answer: none. Even birds know where they're not wanted.

But this was 1995, and in 1995 we still clung to our acronyms, and our conferences too. And so it was: on March

1, 1995 the New York City Gay and Lesbian Community Services Center hosted a forum that, among other things, formally introduced GLHPA to the Gs and Ls whom the organization claimed, at least acronymically, to represent, and whose sex lives it was trying to regulate. Here was Duncan Osborne, who had once written for the now-defunct gay and lesbian newsweekly *OutWeek*, and who, more recently, had written in the *Daily News*: "Impaired by alcohol or drugs, driven by denial or desire for sexually charged ask no questions anonymity, [gay men] are returning to dangerous practices. If this was insane in 1980, I do not know the word for it in 1994." Here was Michelangelo Signorile, already well-known as the FUCKING! MEDIA! CRITIC! for *OutWeek* and, more recently, as the author of *Queer in America*, who, on February 26, 1995, had written on the editorial page of the *New York Times*, "it seems that some of what we did for those who are positive was at the expense of those who are desperately trying to remain negative." And here was Gabriel Rotello, once editor-in-chief of *OutWeek*, later "Cityscape" columnist for *New York Newsday*: "Death waits in New York City's unsafe sex clubs for many a gay soul tonight. Beneath the averted eyes of the local AIDS establishment, the band in New York plays on."

I mention the *OutWeek* connection because I also worked there, for the last fifty-four of the magazine's 105 issues, during which time I had the unenviable task of copyediting Rotello's weekly editorial—unenviable not just because to suggest to Gabriel Rotello that he had conjugated a verb incorrectly was to suggest that one was looking for a new job, but also because his *OutWeek* editorials were guilty of the same bombast that later showed up in his "Cityscape" columns. For example, Gabriel Rotello on morality: "Those who are HIV-positive have an absolute responsibility to protect others." Or Gabriel Rotello on history: "We have evolved from almost complete intolerance of commercial multipartner sex (1986), to muted tolerance as long as it was scrupulously safe (1987–1988), to denial and confusion when it entered the gray zone of possibly unsafe (1989), to indifference when it became blatantly unsafe (1990–today)." Sex clubs, Rotello declared, either "maintain an attitude of brotherly concern for their patrons' health," or they are "AIDS killing grounds." Cf.: "I witnessed a sex murder/suicide last Thursday night." Presumably what Rotello is referring to here is unprotected anal intercourse, and as I tried to figure out how he'd managed to confirm the lack of a condom on the top's dick in the dim confines of a sex room, I found myself imagining Rotello lying on a sticky floor like a dedicated porn cinematographer, squinting up at a pair of swinging balls. And I couldn't help but wonder: did Rotello have pen and paper with him to take notes at the crucial moment, or was there perhaps something else in his hand?

OF COURSE, THERE was no reason to expect a gay tabloid journalist to write with more sensitivity or intelligence than his straight peers on a subject that has long divided the gay community—it's doubtful that a single measured statement has ever fallen from the lips of Larry Kramer about anonymous sex or the epidemic (or anything else having to do with gay life), and if he hadn't opened his big mouth then millions of people who are alive today would have died years ago. But the sensationalism to which Rotello continually resorted led some to question his qualifications to comment on both the issue and the people he wrote about, especially given the political climate into which he dropped his incendiary missives. Because this was 1995, as I mentioned before: the Dinkins idyll was over. Rudy Giuliani had taken office, and, flush with tax revenues from Silicon Alley and Wall Street, the city's first Republican mayor since John Lindsay was attempting to create a kinder, gentler New York, complete with so-called "quality of life" laws that turned certain neighborhoods into de facto gated communities on weekend nights. The primary focus of his administration's attention, however, was the transformation of Times Square into a Disneyfied theme park, but in order to pave the way for family-friendly new businesses the city had first to do away with the old. In the case of Times Square, that meant porn theaters and strip clubs, along with the prostitutes and drug dealers who tended to congregate near them, and, in 1995, the City Council passed a set of "strict new zoning rules" to regulate sex-related businesses, which required them to be more than 500 feet from homes, schools, houses of worship, and, most important, each other, which is to say: the new New York City would no longer have a red-light district. According to the regulations, "An adult eating or drinking establishment is an eating or drinking establishment that regularly features one or more of the following: (1) live performances that are characterized by an emphasis on 'specified anatomical areas' or 'specified sexual activities'; or, (2) films, motion pictures, videocassettes, slides or other photographic reproductions that are characterized by an emphasis upon the depiction or description of 'specified sexual activities' or 'specified anatomical areas.'" The ostensible targets of these regulations were porn theaters and strip joints, and the initial focus of enforcement was Times Square, Hell's Kitchen, and the adjacent neighborhoods. But it didn't take a lawyer to realize that sex clubs and back rooms throughout the city could be—and indeed were—closed down under this rubric. As an organization calling itself Queerwatch wrote, "New York City Council and Mayor Giuliani want to make history out of most of New York City's 'adult' businesses," and as a consequence the timing of statements like those made by Rotello, Signorile, and Osborne was, to use Queerwatch's word, "nightmarish." Of the motivations that informed such statements, the organization wrote, "There is more than a little stupidity, lack of imagination, hypocrisy, and career advancement involved." This charge was all but confirmed when, at the March 1 forum, Gabriel Rotello admitted that if he wrote on other issues he received little or no response—it was only when he wrote on sex clubs that he got a reaction.

Ideological affiliation aside, no one was denying that some gay men were having unprotected sex, whether in public venues or the privacy of their homes. But the reality of HIV prevention requires more than theorizing, monitors, or laws: it requires condoms, and perhaps the most tangible product of the March 1, 1995 forum at the Gay and Lesbian Community Services Center was a second forum, this one held March 18, entitled "Talk Sex," in which participants tried to find out why some gay men weren't suiting up all the time and, more important, how they could be persuaded to. I attended this forum, but because its conveners asked journalists not to take notes and not to report anything said on the panels, and because I consider the fact that I didn't identify myself as a journalist a tacit agreement to abide by those conditions (I was covering the conference for the *Voice*), I won't talk about what was said there.

I'll talk instead about shoes.

There were, when I counted, thirty-four people in my panel, three of whom were moderators and at least two of whom were observers—me, and one of the two women in the room. Of these thirty-four people, at least ten were wearing black boots—primarily the calf-height sponge-soled Doc Martens we all wore in 1987 and 1988 and 1989, which is to say, during the first few years of ACT UP and Queer Nation. At least half a dozen were wearing cross-trainers like the ones Nancy "I'm-going-to-Disneyland!" Kerrigan had hawked incessantly during the previous winter's Olympics; several

were less interested in potential new treatments or the persistence of pre-AIDS sexual behavior than in what Greg Louganis had been thinking as a doctor stitched up his bleeding head at the 1988 Olympics, and how did it feel to win his third and fourth gold medals in Seoul! AIDS had become the issue movie: *An Early Frost, Longtime Companion, Philadelphia, Boys on the Side.* AIDS had become, bizarrely, a cheerful expression of cultural kitsch: when in May of that year I met with Michael Warner in the Big Cup cafe in Chelsea to discuss his article and the events it had engendered, I was distracted by a banner that hung on the opposite side of Eighth Avenue. "Paul Freely," it read, "wishes you a Happy AIDS Awareness Day." (The contemporary version of this sign would be the 54,178 people on Facebook who, as of June 2, 2013, like AIDS.) This normalizing of AIDS, or, more accurately, this normalizing of the terms with which we discussed AIDS—tanned, buff Greg Louganis sitting opposite Oprah Winfrey, with frequent cutaways to him in his Speedo, as opposed to the waiting room full of emaciated men I encountered when I went to my doctor's office—had the opposite of its intended effect: it didn't make AIDS more visible but, rather, rendered it invisible by incorporating it into the realm of things we expected to encounter on a daily basis, and thus need not give our full attention. Viewed in this context, unprotected sex seemed as inevitable and inconsequential as stubbing your toe on a misplaced chair—or, in the CDC's remarkably blasé analysis: "Additionally, many young MSM may underestimate their personal risk for HIV."

Additionally.

And counting.

6

October 4, 1989, 12:39 P.M.

Ladies and Gentlemen, please: Robert Glück is alive! Yes, we say, alive. Now, what does one do w/ that knowledge? Well, for starters, one skips on down to A Different Light and purchases Reader, *Mr. Glück's new book. Of short stories, a novel, essays? Who knows? But look, I thought the man was dead. I mean, I have no idea how true or fictional* Jack the Modernist *or* Elements of a Coffee Service *is, but he uses the first person, he calls himself Bob, he refers to past stories in present ones. He sure makes them seem real. And you know, if he did all the stuff he said he did, then, well, there's a good chance that he could've been dead. I suppose I want to chat w/ the guy, say Hey, I was afraid you were dead, but that may be too prying. Still, might be nice to establish a brief rapport with the guy, w/ another author, an odd one to be sure, but a good one.*

So that's that.

Sat Aug. 4, 1990

Needle Ex.
10:30–2

Bleach kits (Start 82) (34 in Park) (13 left over) (69 out)

Needles 419 (30 to Brooklyn) (109 to Park) (70 left)

Needles in
~~HHT~~ ~~HHT~~ ~~HHT~~ ~~HHT~~ ~~HHT~~
~~HHT~~ ~~HHT~~ ~~HHT~~ ~~HHT~~ ~~HHT~~
~~HHT~~ ~~HHT~~ ~~HHT~~ ~~HHT~~ ~~HHT~~
~~HHT~~ ~~HHT~~ ~~HHT~~ ~~HHT~~ ~~HHT~~
~~HHT~~ ~~HHT~~ ~~HHT~~ ~~HHT~~ ~~HHT~~

Bleach kits: 69 out
Needles: 319 out (109 in Park)
Needles in: 198 in

Zoe, J-C, Allison, me, Sharon (Gerry & Nolan on video)

Cops at table when we arrived; left before we set up. Mob scene at park; one man threatened to take our needles. J-C and Nolan found needles in playground & got video footage. Rick showed up, virtually ODing; Z. & J-C cleaned him up, I gave him $3 that had been donated to us by a client.

Pink Panthers
5:30 →

Nov. 12, 1990

My only note on workshop today: S Koch laughed at S Graham's fag joke. Why am I not surprised?

1/16/91

He said to me yesterday, What bothers? concerns? worries you most about seeing? dating? sleeping with an HIV-positive person? I said, That you'll die. He said, But isn't there anything more immediate? I said, You mean that I'll get infected? No, that doesn't really bother me.

[Later]

I said, Do you mean that you'll get sick? That to me, is just part of the fear that you'll die.

We said other things too, but this was the amazing thing. That here we were, 2 23-year-olds, and we were talking about the impending death of one of them. I've been getting this feeling in the last day— and I've only known Derek for six days, so I still measure time in increments like days, hours—I've been getting this feeling that since we've done such a good job talking about the issues we should now be spared having to deal with them. I.e., Derek shouldn't get AIDS, shouldn't be HIV-positive. I've been getting that feeling, and I've been getting it in such a way that I believe it—I believe Derek is completely healthy, I believe he'll live forever. I feel justified in using that word.

And, too, during this same day I've thought about Derek dead, or in the hospital. Every drug we discussed tonight at T&D—I wondered, Can this help him? Will this keep him alive?

I know how I am. I've always known. I've known (how funny to repeat that word) Derek for 6 days, yet already I've made of him so much. God, I like him. I'm only awaiting his permission to fall in love. Am I ridiculous? I question myself, rather than just write it: I am ridiculous. Derek and I do not understand the same world, we don't understand the world in the same way. But I know myself, I know immediately if I like someone, and I like Derek. But what I never know is, Does he like me? He's so fucking low-key, and I want to demand responsiveness—I want to demand that he fall for me as quickly as I'm falling for him. What is the bottom line? I am—and probably should be considered as such—a distraction from his one purpose in life, which is keeping himself alive. I would be insanely selfish to try to interject myself into his life. This doesn't change the fact that I want him. It just makes me realize that he has to want me, and he has to choose to what extent I'll be in his life.

God, how big that word gets in this context.

Nov. 19, 1991

This man came into the store today. He was about 30, black, & his clothes & his teeth suggest that he was very poor, & he tried to steal a little packet of potpourri. Potpourri. There's something sad about that, that he went for a little thing that only cost $7 & smelled good, as opposed to something like Calvin Klein underwear, a status symbol, or an expensive sweater that he could sell for cash. But he went for something that, I think, he wanted. I wonder if he is homeless; I wonder what he would use to burn it in. I can imagine him opening the plastic & staring at the small leaves & cedar needles, & pressing it close to his face & getting only the most faint whiff of, of what? A forest? A season? A memory?

He couldn't read; he'd never be able to find out that he was supposed to soak the potpourri in water, & then heat the mixture, to release the smell. He tried to read "Paul Smith"; he said "Pierre Cardin" & I think that's only because the way both designers write their names is similar, & Pierre Cardin has been around for so long.

Oh, his teeth. All the poor people who come into this store have bad teeth. His were brown, & he'd apparently lost several in back because the ones in front had spaces as large as teeth between them. That's just so terrible, I think, it's one of the little things that makes poverty really unbearable: looking into the mirror & smiling & being revolted, seeing all the decay of your life manifested in your face in a display of happiness, & knowing that the world sees this as well.

It's dark out & and it's warm, & I'm still a little lost. The world isn't making much sense to me today, as usual, time is moving forward a little too quickly, & what I'm thinking about is Derek dying, & me growing old. It's silly to think of both of these things on the same day, let alone in the same hour. It's silly all the things you can think about at once. Mike "you-should-know-I-have-a-lover" Mogensen came by today, and I do wish I could get to know him better. He's good at little touches, a tap on my knee when he asked me how I was, & there's that delicacy & strength about his body, that pliancy & resiliancy [sic], the idea that he'll bend for a long time before he'll break. "Look at the faces," the subway graffito read, "they are etched w/ the misery of their existence." Who is the person who wrote that? Is he some college-educated smart-ass who read FM Ford's line "The record of human existence is a record of sorrow" [sic], or is he some poor man who got caught trying to steal a box of potpourri?

Oh, now I'm making social commentary & I was just trying to describe Mike. Well he did get dicked out of his job today, a combination of someone's carelessness & some boss's ruthless attitude as s/he decided to try to play parent & teach him a lesson by depriving him of a week's salary. I mean, what's he supposed to eat on for the week, his good looks? I think we've almost reached a stage in history where it's become impossible to talk about social injustices of that kind because they're just so obvious & widespread that anything an artist could say about them is already apparent to his or her audience. At least, that's how I feel when I see most political art. Tell me something I don't know, I want to say.

An observation: a pair of men who are a couple walk slower than a pair of men are who are just friends.

March 30, 1992

ACT UP:

(Just as a by the way: don't forget about your ideas for [1] different color tape on foam core or plexiglass & [2] the lumber yard thingy.)

April 8: Picket by patients @ the Terence Cardinal Cooke Care Center

Re: Eric Sawyer on the Antonio Pagan et al zap. The rhetoric at this meeting is still incredible. The VV flyer they handed out said as much and more than he did;

why can't we even talk to each other w/o resorting to propaganda? Our language isn't our own anymore, it seems; we don't even trust ourselves to tell the plain truth.

There's someone crying at the back of the room. That's why we're here, isn't it?

June 15, 1993

There's a serial murderer loose on the streets of London, & he's targeting gay men. According to a *Times* reporter who called me today to ask for my opinion on "how the homosexual community opens themselves to this kind of thing": (note: I've no idea how she found out I was here), the killer is actually more specific: he's going after men in S/M bars, or into S/M. I'm not sure what she expected of me, though from her comments she seems to have deduced from M&J that I'm into S/M (good for her), but I'm afraid I said something terribly, terribly stupid, since she woke me from my jet-lag nap when she called. I haven't yet seen any reports in the gay press, so I don't know what their take will be. Someone's been calling the *Sun* claiming to be the killer, and claiming that he'll go on killing at the rate of one a week; whether this is the real killer, or just someone trying to spur him on, remains to be seen.

parades, the meetings in the Gay and Lesbian Community Services Center and the Great Hall at Cooper Union and in apartments scattered around the East Village and Lower East Side (this last blurs the line into sex)—I see it through a scrim of despair and failure, the former understandable, the latter less so, given the profound changes so soon to come, and the pivotal role ACT UP played in bringing them about. This disconnect has long puzzled me because, despite the global nature of the plague—despite 34 million HIV-positive people in the world, and nearly three million new infections each year, not to mention almost two million deaths—we beat the epidemic here. In America, I mean, in New York, or at least in my circle of friends. People stopped dropping dead is what I mean, and many of the people who continue to die are victims of extenuating circumstances as much as HIV: of addiction, and broken health care, and an increasingly stratified educational system that's created a permanent and disempowered underclass. But still. We won. The AIDS wards are empty, the streets aren't lined with walking corpses.

But even as I write that I think of a pair of my friends named Alan Rivers and Byron Clayton, and the first time I tried to save someone by writing about him—about them in this case—or at least to save a piece of them in the event that the epidemic claimed their lives. They were one of those gay couples whose fraternal resemblance made a certain kind of homophobe especially uncomfortable. Both were pale and wiry with brown crewcut hair, Alan five-eight, Byron five-seven, and both had pierced nipples as well; in the years before every block in the Village sported a tattoo parlor and piercing shop, I think they did each other's. I saw Byron's one night when he changed his shirt for a Pink Panthers patrol and a light caught the silver rings, making them flash on his chest ("Did they hurt?" I'd asked him; "Yes!" was his terse reply), but didn't learn of Alan's until Byron told me how his lover's X-rays had been the talk of St. Vincent's. Doctors and nurses came from all over, pediatrics, geriatrics, OB/GYN, to see the two perfect circles that stood out clearly despite a backdrop of dark, fluid-filled lungs. At that point it was just pneumonia, but by the following week it was clearly *Pneumocystis carinii*, and yes, Byron told me, he had tested positive as well. They'd been tested together, but Alan's PCP diagnosis beat the lab by a week. To my mind, it was as though someone had whispered in Byron's ear, You have seven, eight years to live, and in Alan's, You have three. But the epidemic understood better than I that these numbers were means, that some people lived longer than this, others not so long. Which is to say: Alan was dead in a little over a year, Byron in two.

Now, as I read over what little I managed to get down on paper twenty-three years ago, I see that the only aspects of Alan and Byron's lives I recorded were those the epidemic intersected, and as such my words feel like a testament to AIDS rather than to the people it affected, the lives it claimed. I understand why this happened, though it doesn't make me feel any better: Alan and Byron were the first people I knew to discover that they were HIV-positive after I'd met them. We met in ACT UP and had only known each other six weeks before Alan was hospitalized, and for two of those weeks I didn't see him because he was tired, Byron told us: he was run-down, he had a bad cold, we're not sure what's wrong, he's in the hospital, he has AIDS. Shortly before, during a midnight picnic—Alan, Byron, me, Jean-Claude—Alan had told us how beat he'd been lately, how he couldn't catch his breath after climbing a flight of stairs. You're thirty, we'd told him, these things happen when you turn thirty. Join a gym, increase your lung power, meet hot men. No one mentioned the A-word—including Alan, though we knew he was trying to tell us he thought he had it. We were all AIDS activists, but still we pushed it away, because AIDS, like any disease, wears the faces of those it affects, and it was easier to fight—less emotional, certainly—when the enemy wasn't human. This isn't the talk show message, of course. The producers of talk shows and human-interest segments on the evening news believe that by putting a face on the epidemic they rouse viewer sympathy—and they do, and that's the problem. HIV (or cancer, or a miscarriage, or a divorce, or a box office flop) becomes a life lesson, the proverbial blessing in disguise, the window God opens when he closes a door, each bromide making HIV that much more benign, until it starts to seem not like something that should be avoided or resisted but something that should practically be embraced, a distinction, a gift even, a badge of honor and a path to wisdom, viz., Andrew Sullivan's declaration near the end of 1996: "It allowed me to see things that I had never been able to see before." During the four- or five-year period when AIDS was the focus of my political and artistic life, and consequently my social and sexual life, I did my best to keep the disease and those it affected separate in my mind, because I didn't want to fall into the trap of fighting for one person I knew, or even a hundred or a thousand people I knew, lest when those battles were won or lost (*absit omen*) I should make the mistake of thinking that the war itself had been won or lost. Which, of course, is exactly what happened.

Or maybe I just wanted to insulate myself from tragedy, from pain. In my life, these things happened to other people. My mother died shortly before my fourth birthday, my father's three subsequent marriages were full of heartache and turmoil. But I always understood it as *his* heartache and turmoil, and at some point over the course of my first two decades came to conceive of myself as a bit player in someone else's misery, an Ishmael, a Marlowe, a Lockwood, a John Dowell from *The Good Soldier*: a witness whose fate is to be the medium of other people's tragedies, not recognizing until too late that the stories he's telling are also his own, or that being a witness is as much a life as being a hero or victim. This sense of myself only grew stronger when I moved to New York and joined ACT UP and, after meeting several people my age who were HIV-positive, realized that my health had been protected partly by geography (I lived in central Kansas until 1985, where HIV had yet to make deep inroads) but also by fear: because of the ephemeral (to me) threat of HIV, and the more palpable menace of homophobia, I didn't come out until I was nineteen, didn't lose my virginity until a year later, in 1988, by which time the tenets of safe sex were well known, and undoubtedly saved my life. Although there was a little luck involved too, by which I mean that I was so nervous the first time I got fucked that I didn't use a condom—didn't even *think* about using a condom—which scared the shit out of me, just as his own unsafe encounter had so rattled Michael Warner in 1995. It would be the last time I had unprotected sex for nineteen years, until I got engaged in 2007.

"It seems to me I know more about fear than I do pain," I wrote in 1990, "and I don't want to add Alan and Byron's pain to my fear." This statement strikes me as just as true in 2013 as it did twenty-three years ago, but what it's taken me all this time to realize is that much of "their" fear was a projection of my own. It was Byron who taught me to yell "ACT UP! Fight back! Fried eggs!" (instead of "ACT UP! Fight back! Fight AIDS!") to relieve the monotony of two- or three-hour chants at demos: you could shout it right in cops' faces, in reporters'; they never heard the difference. His biggest gripe: that he and Alan didn't learn their status sooner. He could've *died*, Byron told me in the hospital, he could've been monitoring his T cells, he could've been prophylaxing months ago, he could've *died*. The emphasis in his words was on tense, not meaning, as if the threat of death had been removed by mere knowledge that it existed (I would make the same rational-izations a year later, when I dated an HIV-positive man for the first time). But they weren't deluded—not anymore. I could drop dead tomorrow, Alan told me from his hospital bed, pentamidine dripping into his arm, but I feel myself getting better and I just can't think every second that I'm dying, I'd go crazy. I remember hoping it would be that simple: that Alan and Byron would only think of their deaths when one of them got sick, and that I, too, would only think of their deaths when one of them got sick. I remember trying to create an elaborate metaphor to explain the difference between my knowledge and theirs—something to the effect that death, embodied in the hospital, was a land I only visited, clutching my green plastic visitor's card like a passport, but that they inhabited. But the truth was simpler: there were times when I woke sweating from the AIDS nightmare we all had in 1990 and knew it had only been a dream, and there were nights when they woke sweating and didn't know—they just didn't know.

I remember this one time . . . Fuck. That's how you talk about dead people, isn't it, after the emotions have dulled and the specifics faded. After twenty-three years have gone by. "I remember this one time," you say, knowing that at the time it hadn't been an "experience" or a memory, let alone a symbol. It had been life. Yours. Theirs. You store away the mnemonic thinking it will help you remember, and indeed it does: but the first thing it brings to mind is always itself, and as more and more time goes by you have to work harder and harder to get to the truth that lies beyond the signpost. But even so. I remember this one time. Spring 1990. Byron and I were bicycling down Twenty-second Street between Eleventh and Tenth avenues, which was then a block of derelict warehouses and garages, many shrouded in scaffolding that had itself fallen into disrepair; Alan was home from the hospital, sleeping. Two fast revolutions and we coasted, standing on the pedals, for fifty feet. Sweat dripped down my back, but not from exertion. Some unknown zoning consideration had decreed that traffic should run west to east on this single block, rather than east to west as it did on other even-numbered streets, which meant that cars couldn't continue on from the block of 22nd between Ninth and Tenth, leaving the block between Tenth and Eleventh virtually devoid of vehicular traffic, and, at night, of pedestrians as well. Gay men had taken advantage of this desolation to transform the block into a cruising strip. Men lined the sidewalks, alone, in pairs, larger groups. Where sex was happening, it was usually just hand-jobs, circle jerks. A couple of men knelt before their partners. One man, still sitting on his bicycle, stared us down as we passed, seemingly ignorant of the man who stroked his penis. When Byron and I reached Tenth Avenue, we kissed good-bye, waited for the light to change. He surprised me then: "The worst thing about being positive," he said, "is that in the last eight years I've only had unsafe sex three times." This floored me. There was, on the one hand, the idea that it only took three slips to catch him; there was, on the other, the idea that for the previous eight years Byron had known that a single unprotected encounter could leave him infected. I shook my head in silence, we parted. Having tested negative since I'd moved to New York, I never connected his actions to my own unsafe encounter.

But Byron pulled me aside a few days later. "I went back after you left, Dale," he told me. "I told myself I was just going for a look, but there was this big ol' Daddy and I couldn't help myself. He wanted me to go home with him but I wanted it right there on the street." "What did you do?" "I gave him the ultimate safe-sex blowjob." "What's that?" "I made him keep his pants on." "Did he come?" "Did he come!" "How?" And as he described it to me, a sly smile creeping across his face, told me how he'd licked the man's pants until they were sopping, I felt a barrier between us similar to the cotton covering that Daddy's crotch, because I realized that not only was Byron's tragedy not my tragedy, but neither was it my triumph. I was only listening in, looking on, empathizing perhaps, but not really understanding. And though I've never forgotten what he told me, as the years go by I find myself wondering more and more if the words I remember are still his, or if, by now, they belong only to me.

8

Amebiasis first.

Then hepatitis.

NSU—nonspecific urethritis. That was kind of a bitch.

When my doctor's office took a swab, the Q-tip in my urethra was less uncomfortable than the effort to avoid an erection while the hot nurse practitioner "milked" my penis to push what little discharge there was toward the tip. He sent the sample to the lab but went ahead and prescribed the treatment for gonorrhea, which cleared up the symptoms for a week. But then the symptoms came back and I had to go through a second round of antibiotics, whose effect on my gastroenterological system was significantly more unpleasant than the burn when I took a piss.

Anal warts. I protested to my doctor that I had only ever had a bare dick up my ass the one time, and that had been three years earlier, so how could I have suddenly contracted warts? My doctor couldn't quite keep the smirk off his face. Have you had a finger up there? he asked. "Asked." Lesson learned.

I discovered I was immune to hep B when I went for my vaccination—i.e., I'd already been exposed.

Another UTI. This from a new boyfriend who didn't realize he was harboring an infection. He didn't realize he was HIV-positive either, but awkwardly enough I did, when he told me that the results of his test (his first) had been "delayed" for a week, which those of us who knew the drill understood as code for a positive result that had been sent out for confirmation. Man, that was a long week. The next three years were a breeze by comparison.

Genital warts welcomed me back to single life.

When I got crabs when I was thirty-five I was like, I can't believe you waited so long! They made quite an entrance though—I discovered them on the plane back from Barcelona. Sorry, Delta!

Scabies was the last of them, which felt like appropriate closure, since I'd also had it as a kid. My slutty days were over by the time syphilis came back in fashion, though how I missed herpes I'll never know.

For a few years after that a wart would show up like a birthday card from a forgetful aunt. I won't say it was fun having them frozen off, but, you know, it could have been worse. Safe sex works!

(N.B. potential critics: you are not allowed to use the headline "Warts and All" in reviews of this book.)

9

The Townhouse is an old man's restaurant on the Upper East Side of Manhattan. The Townhouse is, more specifically, an old gay man's restaurant, one that has survived epochal shifts in government, epidemiology, and fashion for going on thirty years. Also, the food is not good. In 1993, when I visited it for the first and only time, the place was frequented by white-haired gentlemen who favored pleated khakis and double-breasted navy blazers brass-buttoned loosely over large stomachs, and, judging by the pictures on its website, it still is. The Townhouse, in other words, was not (and, to the best of my knowledge, is not) a particularly remarkable place, save that, discounting the ATM where Thomas Mulcahy withdrew money at 11:30 P.M. on July 7, 1992, it was the last place he was known to have been alive, and so I went there a year and six weeks after Mulcahy died, dragging my friend Bruce with me because I wanted the company, and because we were eating on the *Voice*'s dime.

We were the only patrons in the dining room who were under thirty. Just inside the door of the restaurant was a vestibule with a small bar where a couple of younger men sat nursing cocktails. Bruce and I were given a curious glance by the bartender when we walked past these men to the dining room; were scrutinized again by a waiter, who went to fetch the maître d'; were given the once-over and then virtually dismissed by the maître d' as he led us to a table. The dining room was busy but not crowded. The lights were tastefully, one wants to say mercifully, dim, the walls the color of parched earth and hung with several brightly colored paintings of flowers by someone called Russ Elliott— paintings that, Bruce remarked, looked like they ought to have been posters. A pair of women we took to be a lesbian couple sat at one table and, at two others, an apparently gay man dined with an apparently straight woman. The other eight or nine occupied tables were exclusively gay, including three at which only one man sat. All three of these single men ate slowly. None of them seemed to have brought anything to occupy himself while he ate, and instead looked around the room with the docile patience of a cow at the cud. One of these men sat next to Bruce on the banquette that ran the length of one wall. This man was in his fifties, plump, carefully manicured, and wearing a navy blue blazer over a navy blue polo with cardinal red stripes, and he had a matching navy and cardinal handkerchief tucked in the breast pocket of his navy blue jacket. (Did I already say his jacket was navy blue? He was wearing a *lot* of blue.) Bruce and I were discussing the book Bruce had been reading on the subway when, with the flourish of a magic trick, the man beside him produced a clothbound dustjacketless copy of *The Art of Ernest Hemingway*. The man held the book in front of him at the unnatural angle that people in commercials hold boxes of tampons or packages of breath mints, which is to say, so that we could see it better than he could. He looked at the front cover of the book, which was blank, and he looked at the back cover of the book, which was also blank, and then he looked, randomly, at three or four pages inside the book (which could have been blank for all the interest he showed them), and then, when neither Bruce nor I had said anything to him about his book, he put it down on the bench beside him, almost under Bruce's hip, and ate his meal without looking at it, or us, again. To this day, I don't know if the book was by Ernest Hemingway, or about him.

The staff grew noticeably more friendly when we ordered a bottle of wine, and when we ordered appetizers before our main course, and when, by chance, we ordered some of the higher-priced items on the menu, and by the time Bruce ordered dessert we were being treated just like the other men who were there for dinner, which, I assume, we were not at first taken to be. The Townhouse, as I mentioned before, is generally regarded as a hustler bar. A friend of mine who worked there as a waiter in the early nineties (and who, as chance would have it, later became a call boy, claiming Richard Simmons and Gianni Versace among his clients) told me this wasn't true; what was true, he told me, was that unaccompanied young men would sometimes sit at the bar for four or five hours, nursing drinks and chatting in a very pleasant manner with just about anyone who tried to speak with them, as long as that person was not another unaccompanied young man. The men eating alone in the dining room were apparently unaware of this, or the men eating alone in the dining room were not interested in the unaccompanied young men drinking at the bar, or the men eating alone in the dining room wanted to fill themselves with food before they filled themselves with the unaccompanied young men at the bar—or, perhaps, the men eating alone simply enjoyed eating alone, and the unaccompanied young men were simply very friendly, as long as you were not another unaccompanied young man.

The only reason I went to the Townhouse, of course, was to see where Thomas Mulcahy met his killer. Like any aspiring journalist, I believed it was necessary to place the two of them *in situ* in order to understand them better, or at least better (read: more vividly) describe what had

happened to them. But being in the Townhouse only rein-
forced how little I knew about Mulcahy, let alone his killer,
and the best I could do was to place the former in the body
of the man who didn't read *The Art of Ernest Hemingway*,
which led to the epistemologically uncomfortable position
of placing the killer in Bruce's body, or my own. It was the
same sense of dislocation I'd felt in the Phoenix in Milwaukee, when the Latino hustler's hate-filled stare made me
realize that my skin color marked me out as john rather
than prostitute and at the same time rendered that transac-
tion invisible to official scrutiny. And however repulsive the
feeling might have been, it was also intoxicating, especially
in the wake of Jeffrey Dahmer's successful exploitation of
the overlapping prejudices of the straight and gay and black
and white milieux he moved through, not invisibly, no, but
with the mirrored camouflage of someone adept at hiding
behind other people's projections of normality. (It's worth
remembering that Dahmer wasn't apprehended until Tracy
Edwards, a black man who'd escaped from Dahmer's apartment, returned with two cops, who accompanied Edwards
because their keys couldn't open the handcuffs attached to
Edwards's wrist; even then, Dahmer was only taken into
custody after one of the cops went into the bedroom to look
for the knife Edwards said Dahmer had threatened him with
and found Polaroids of Dahmer's victims.) In the Townhouse, the equation was flipped. Here, it was my youth
rather than my race that had been made strange to me,
given additional or at any rate previously unrealized power.

sex: the lure, the chase, the catch. I could imagine the man who didn't read *The Art of Ernest Hemingway* rubbing his belly too, not because he'd renounced the hunt, but because he understood that cash trumped the primacy of bodies in the sexual hierarchy, at least in the milieu in which he'd chosen to troll. And yes, I realize I've reversed my position: have recast myself from predator to victim, ceded my connection with Jeffrey Dahmer to the man who didn't read *The Art of Ernest Hemingway* or, who knows (Richard Rogers was still unknown at the time I was reporting this story, after all, still at large), to the very man who had killed Thomas Mulcahy. This epistemological uncertainty—arbitrariness really—stayed with me after I left the Townhouse, made me uncomfortable as I attempted to write up what had happened for my *Voice* article. I'd always understood that journalism and memoir entailed a certain amount of projection, but I'd never realized how much role-playing is involved. How much the whole enterprise resembles a game. I suppose the tendency is more universal—we all make snap judgments, after all, or pretend to be a little better or worse than we really are—but journalism exacerbates these tendencies, if it doesn't simply rely on them. Give us more color, my editor said when I turned in my piece. Give us more atmosphere. Let the reader know who these people really are. But of course I had no idea who these people really were, and, what's more, I didn't care: not about the man who didn't read *The Art of Ernest Hemingway*, nor, for that matter, about Thomas Mulcahy. Not because they were unimportant had picked up his victims in bars that I spent a fair bit of time in, not because I was reporting the story (I wouldn't be contacted by the *Voice* until I returned to New York in August) but because I liked spending time in bars like the ones in which Colin Ireland was said to have found his victims. Bars like the Coleherne, the Anvil, the Backstreet, the Block, the Shipwrights Arms—bars that in New York would be called leather bars but in London are more commonly referred to as dress-code bars because they insist on appropriate attire, be it bleachers and braces or chaps, harness, and dog collar, with the same prudent zeal with which 1950s country clubs insisted on jackets and ties. Unlike the New York murders, there was, for me, a sexual ambiguity in the London murders that wasn't based on race or youth but instead on a straightforward erotic affinity with both the killer and his real and potential victims, and this ambiguity, this affinity, checked my pen whenever I tried writing about what had happened. Exposing men who concealed themselves in a costume of leather or rubber or military uniform or skin regalia to set themselves apart not just from the average straight person or the average gay person but, if only for a few hours, their average, everyday selves in order to engage in a stylized pick-up and sexual ritual that might involve blindfolds, gags, bondage, role-playing, pissing, shitting, bloodletting, fistfucking, asphyxiation, and no small amount of pain—open palms, closed fists, boots, belts, crops, whips, clamps, needles, brands—meant writing about things that I had done or might do, and that I did to culturally, through the hallowed milieux of leather bars, but also via paraphilias, which, because they flout the conventional associations of this or that object or behavior or environment, assault not just the physical senses but good taste, propriety, the very idea of culture, and make it possible, if only for a few endorphin-charged moments, to pervert the homogenization and commodification of modern life, whose greedy grasp extends increasingly into the realm of personality itself. Late twentieth-century capitalism had a prurient fascination with all things sexual but offered little by way of approval or condemnation as long as money could be made. And for better or worse, money erases cultural and moral distinctions. We may not have been equal in the eye of the law in 1993, but we were all the same in the eye of the market. Even so, there were still some gay men who wanted to think of themselves as different from other people, gay as well as straight—not necessarily "abject," in Michael Warner's phrase, let alone "anticommunal," in Leo Bersani's (although not necessarily *not* abject either, or communal for that matter), but, more simply, as beings whose identities were bound up in sex— *but only while they were having it.* Gore Vidal maintained until the end of his life that "there is no such thing as a homosexual or a heterosexual person. There are only homo- or heterosexual acts," and to the degree that that's true, then the men in the bars where Colin Ireland found his victims recreated themselves in some fundamental way when they took off their workaday drag and replaced it with leather or rubber, exchanged their given names for Sir or boy, trumped cognition with acts of physical stimuli that for the seconds or minutes or hours they could be borne recast the entire body as a single Foucauldian sexual organ. The freedom granted by these experiences is fragile at best, if not simply illusory (sex that requires specialized and often expensive accessories would seem to be the very definition of a commodified activity), but the contradiction didn't detract from its appeal. It did, however, make its participants—its adherents, I want to say, its believers—wary in the way they shared their experiences, because separating them from the context in which they occurred reduced them beyond recognition—or, rather, magnified them into meaningless abstraction.

This, then, was the source of my reticence in writing about the London murders, and I encountered it whenever I tried to talk to someone about the crimes. It certainly wasn't shame, as the massive size of the leather contingent in any gay pride parade demonstrates, not to mention the context in which most of my conversations took place. It wasn't even silence per se. It was, rather, a refusal to integrate certain specifically sexual activities into their nonsexual lives (indeed, the very word "integrate," with its assimilationist connotations, gives away the game, and "incorporate," the other word I considered using, is even worse). These activities could be hinted at or even declared (c.f., pride parades), but the sex that the signs and flags (and chaps and codpieces) signified remained fundamentally unseen and unseeable; unexplained; inexplicable. I remember, for example, a man named Grant I met in the First Out, a gay cafe just off Tottenham Court Road, who, within an hour of meeting me (and still in the cafe), told me how a former boyfriend used to tie him spreadeagle to the bed in the ground-floor bedroom of their house, duct tape one end of a long length of plastic tubing into his mouth, then walk with the other end upstairs to the living room, where he would watch television—*EastEnders*, *Coronation Street*, *Neighbours*—drink beer, and piss through a funnel into the tube all evening long. Not immediately, but over the course of several hours, the piss would make its way to the helpless Grant on the floor below, who, because of the tape sealing his mouth, had no choice but to swallow it. Grant went so far as to tell me that I could buy the tubing, not at a DIY store, let alone a fetish shop, but at a store that sold supplies for aquariums, where it would be less expensive, but he would not tell me that he was a fetishist or into BDSM, and when I pressed him denied that such specific sexual activities constituted an identity as opposed to, say, a predilection, a hobby, something he did every once in a while—once or twice a month, say, or once or twice a day—but to which he didn't devote a great deal of thought otherwise.

Or as my friend Gordon wrote me in December of that year:

> *To finish off, I'll leave you with something special for*
> *Christmas, and try to give a few details of a recent*

sexual encounter in which my behaviour surprized me a bit. Parts of it are blurry, and parts will likely sound cliché, but here it goes. On Saturday night, eve of a full moon, lunar eclipse and "dies mali," I found myself in the only bar I can stand on such a night, on the third of a three-day coke binge. (I should add that I hadn't been out at all for six weeks, due to a mix of moving anxiety, the flu, and disinterest.) It was an extraordinarily friendly night—I think because of the number of Seattlites in town escaping American thanksgiving—and I was pretty friendly myself, with a couple of 'seventies-style' mutual-electric-exchanges.

Early on, I locked eyes with a man I swore I'd never seen before, with a magnificent bare chest, smooth shaven head, scraggly goatee and piercing eyes. Hours later, I realized that he usually sported a Nordic blond crewcut and that I had seen him and his lover many times before but had assumed—hastily, it turns out—that he was less free in his relationship than in his choice of leather and rubber ensembles. I warned him that I was on coke and therefore a bit short-circuited hard-on-wise, but when we went through the list of things we could do, he found good enough reason to shrug off his lover, take me to the pool in the basement of his apartment building, piss all over me and fuck me face-down on the cold tiles in the changing rooms, among other positions and locations. There was more than this, but it's the part that's blurry (sort of) and it's the kind of thing I'm bad at explaining. Anyways, as he reached orgasm, he pulled out and asked if he could come inside me. Bad enough we were fucking without a you-know-what—but my initial objection was admittedly groggy—I was obviously torn over the matter, and after a few strokes of phallic coersion, I gave in to the Bad Deed. The whole experience was more intense and extreme than I can communicate—in fact, I think it was when I stupidly, sluttishly groaned, "Oh god, this is the best" that he was inspired to take the liberty.

So as my mood brightened over the following days ("Sparky's back," quipped a friend), I obsessed over what I had done—before admitting to myself that I was thrilled. I didn't enjoy the dilemma, but I did enjoy the coersion and the strange inner sense of abandon. I also enjoyed my massage therapist's reaction to the large bruise along my spine that I don't remember getting ("Looks like you rubbed up against something there . . ."). I can't put down why I feel such amazement at my own actions and reactions. Only, perhaps, to say there's this feeling of having made a leap in my understanding of myself, not the thing you'd expect from Saturday night at the Shaggy Horse. This state of mind moved me, just yesterday, to finally defy my departed lover's opinions about the

aesthetics of my chest and get a pierce in one of those
resilient nipples of mine. About time.

What unites Graham and Gordon's stories—and, now
that I think about it, Byron's too—is the hyperspecific manner in which they're told, and the way in which that
specificity is employed, not in the service of information,
but the erotic. Graham and Gordon and Byron weren't simply trying to tell me how hot their respective encounters
had been, *they were trying to turn me on*, because it was
only when what they'd done existed in an erotic context
that it could be perceived by an observer in the same way
its participants had—or, not perceived, but *felt*. Experienced, in the loins as well as the head. That there were other
implications to their actions, other meanings that might be
gleaned from them, was undeniable, but also unsayable, viz.
Gordon's *It's the kind of thing I'm bad at explaining . . . The*
whole experience was more intense and extreme than I can
communicate . . . I can't put down why I feel such amaze-
ment . . . Over the course of the last three years of his life
Gordon wrote me dozens of letters amounting to some
50,000 words, almost all of which had something to do
with sex: of course he could have communicated the source
of his amazement: he just refused to. (Six months earlier,
in June, I had recorded this impression of my second date
with Robbie: "I simply can't describe how turned on I was,
& I don't want to try. I really, really don't want to use
words—at least not now—to get at the feelings of that

experience.") Likewise, Graham and I had picked each other out in the vanilla environment of the First Out because of our hair (cropped), our Levi's (too tight, cuffed high up the ankle over our boots), and our jackets (an acetate aviator jacket in his case, a Lewis Leathers biker jacket in mine): not only did our sexual habits constitute an identity, but that identity came with its own uniforms, both informal (what we wore in the First Out) and dress: the more extreme gear we put on to go to leather bars, or just to have sex. And Byron . . .

Byron.

After Alan died, Byron was forced to return to his homophobic family in Australia because he could no longer afford his meds. He sold off many of his possessions before he left, some of them because he couldn't get them to Australia, some because he knew he was going home to die and he didn't want them to end up in his family's hands, or the trash. Some of the stuff he sold to strangers but some was offered only to certain of his friends, and the last time I saw Byron was when he invited me to his apartment and pulled out a suitcase (I think it had been under the bed, but the bed was gone now) and showed me the collection of bondage gear he had made for himself and Alan, and as I sifted through it he told me how, after Alan's funeral, Alan's straight brother had come back to Alan and Byron's apartment and he and Byron had dropped acid and had sex. It was Byron who shaved my head for the first time. He did Jean-Claude's on the same occasion, but only Byron and I had erections. I would have slept with him then, but I wasn't ready to sleep with someone I knew was HIV-positive, and I would have slept with him the last time I saw him, might even have used the four shackles I bought from him, but there was no longer a bed to tie him to. There was no longer a bed, and the bones were visible in his pitifully thin wrists and ankles, and there was a piece of paper taped to the wall beside his toilet listing the frequency and consistency of his bowel movements because he had cryptosporidiosis and was literally shitting his life away, but even so, he wanted to tell me that he had seduced Alan's brother because it was the only way he could communicate the reality of his life with Alan to that man, who was practically a stranger—who referred to Alan by his first name, John, and who paused whenever Byron said the name Alan, as if asking himself who that was. And, of course, it was the closest Byron would ever come to sleeping with Alan again, just as giving me his gear was the only way the pleasure they had shared would live on in this world.

WELL. YOU CAN run with the Dionysian thesis if you want, but if you prefer a simpler explanation for why people in London wouldn't talk to me, or, at any rate, wouldn't talk about certain things, there's also the fact that BDSM occupies a gray zone of British law, which is to say that BDSM itself is not illegal, but many sadomasochistic activities are. (As the Christians say, hate not the sinner but the sin.) As with the (now-unconstitutional) sodomy statutes in the

United States, the law categorizing certain sadomasochistic behaviors as forms of assault ostensibly applies to both heterosexuals and homosexuals, but in practice gay people are prosecuted with greater severity. By far the most notorious example of biased prosecution is known as the Spanner case, from the name given by Manchester police to a sting operation carried out between 1987, when officers found a videotape that depicted several gay men engaging in activities that included "beatings, genital abrasions and lacerations," and 1989, when sixteen men, including several who had been the recipients rather than the perpetrators of the "beatings, genital abrasions and lacerations," were charged with a variety of crimes, among them "assault, aiding and abetting assault, and keeping a disorderly house." The case was initially heard in the Old Bailey in December 1990, when the indicted parties' only defense—that everyone involved had consented to the activities—was ruled ineligible, at which point the men pleaded guilty and were given sentences of up to four and a half years in prison. The convictions were upheld in the High Court in January 1992 (although the sentences were reduced), and upheld again by the House of Lords on March 11, 1993—which is to say, the day after Peter Walker's body was found, and, not surprisingly, the timing of these events hampered London police in their investigation into Peter Walker's murder and the four murders that were soon to follow, as gay men who might have had relevant information refused to contact authorities for fear of being imprisoned themselves.

trying to balance a desire to get laid with the possibility that the man who came up to me in the Backstreet or the Block with a loutish smile on his face and a pair of handcuffs dangling from his belt might be wondering what I looked like, not with a gag in my mouth, but my own severed genitals—which, not surprisingly, is what most of the people I spoke to were also thinking. In the course of these slightly surreal nights (during one of which I met the man I ended up dating for the next three years) I was told all sorts of things, none of which I wrote down and most of which I forgot almost immediately. But the one thing I do remember someone telling me, a man named Andy whom I met at the Block, was that he didn't pay much heed to what the tabloids printed about this serial killer because there had been another serial killer loose in London for twelve years, and they didn't have anything sensible to write about that one either. It didn't really matter to the straight press how we died, Andy said. It just mattered that we were dying. This was not, I think, too harsh a judgment—not for 1993, when queers were still grappling with "the murderous representations of homosexuals unleashed and 'legitimized' by AIDS," as Leo Bersani had put it back in 1987, and possibly not even for 2013, when, as I write, the New York City Police Department is investigating the January 2 murder of David Rangel, the January 28 murder of Charles Romo, and the February 9 murder of Joseph Benzinger, all three of whom appear to have been killed by men they picked up for sex, not to mention the May 17 murder of Mark Carson by Elliot Morales, who, according to witnesses, shouted antigay slurs at Carson on a West Village street before shooting him point-blank in the face, or the ever-increasing cache of YouTube videos of the assaults and murders of gay men in Russia and Nigeria. And if you think it is too harsh, well, fuck you too.

10

"The imagination," James Baldwin wrote in *The Evidence of Things Not Seen*, his take on Wayne Williams and the Atlanta child murders of 1979–1981, "is poorly equipped to accommodate an action in which one, instinctively, recognizes the orgasmic release of self-hatred." Poorly equipped maybe, but fascinated, as evidenced by the ever-proliferating biographies and biopics about serial killers—the crime-scene pictures, the reenactments, the interviews from prison, the tearful, highly compensated testimonials from survivors and relatives and sometimes the killers themselves—not to mention the literary musings of a Dennis Cooper or James Ellroy or Bret Easton Ellis, which, though every bit as visceral as their pulp counterparts, at least dispense with any show of insight and portray their protagonists as manifestations of a violence whose cause is at once external and internal, cultural as well as psychological, and, ultimately, as bland as it is erotic. Which is to say: at some point during the 1970s or 1980s serial murder became a spectator sport, and gay serial killers, with their clueless wives and teenage accomplices, their necrophilia and cannibalism, their clown paintings and torture chambers, their inchoate teenage victims running through impoverished urban neighborhoods "buck naked . . . beaten up . . . very bruised," only to be returned to their murderer by a policeman who couldn't "do anything about somebody's sexual preferences in life," became America's favorite gladiators. For homophobes, gay serial murder was a perfect ouroboros: men like Colin Ireland and Jeffrey Dahmer and the as-yet unidentified Richard Rogers confirmed their worst suspicions about faggots while simultaneously reassuring them that homosexuality was a self-annihilating phenomenon.

And at the same time that gay serial killers were becoming fixtures on televisions and magazine covers and book jackets, PWAs were also becoming increasingly visible in the American media—on talk shows and in movies and a spate of books so numerous that they merited their own category at the Lambda Literary Awards. But despite the obvious sympathy with which most of these narratives were pitched, I viewed them with the same suspicion I viewed media coverage of gay serial killers—as, if not manifestations of a desire to see dead queers, then aesthetic accomplices of same. This was true whether the subject of the story was homosexual or heterosexual. In the former case, AIDS functioned as a reminder that gay men were being punished for the crime of their sexual activities, as when, in *Philadelphia*, Tom Hanks's character confesses that he'd had sex in a porn theater, not a thousand times, not a hundred times, not a dozen times, but "once" (so innocent is Hanks's Andrew Beckett that the only thing he says to his partner as he enters a private booth—besides his name, which is pretty much the last thing someone says at that point in the game—is "Now what do we do?"). If, on the other hand, the subject was heterosexual, it served to incite the "general public"'s hatred of gay men, without whose promiscuity the epidemic would not exist and, more to the point, wouldn't threaten innocents: faithful wives, hemophiliac children, the unsuspecting Samaritans of the health care profession. As Alison Gertz, who believed she contracted HIV from a "bisexual" man, told readers of the *New York Times*, "I'm heterosexual, and it only took one time for me." I don't mean to suggest that Gertz or the makers of *Philadelphia* bore any expressed or even unconscious animosity toward gay men, only that the context in which their stories were presented couldn't help but reinforce the prejudices many people had about the things gay men did, and the consequences of those actions.

Because AIDS, as Simon Watney had told us in *Policing Desire*, in addition to being a medical catastrophe, was "a crisis of representation":

> From very early on in the history of the epidemic, Aids has been mobilised to a prior agenda of issues concerning the kind of society we wish to inhabit.

These include most of the shibboleths of contemporary "familial" politics, including anti-abortion and
anti-gay positions. It is therefore impossible to iso-
late the representation of Aids, or campaigns on
behalf of people with Aids, from this contingent set
of values and debates.

Leo Bersani, in "Is the Rectum a Grave?" pushed Watney's point further: "The persecuting of children of
heterosexuals with AIDS (or who have tested positive for
HIV) is particularly striking in view of the popular description of such people as 'innocent victims.' It is as if gay
men's 'guilt' were the real agent of infection." The children
Bersani referred to in this instance were Ricky, Robert,
and Randy Ray, three HIV-positive brothers who lived in
Arcadia, Florida, and who had been kicked out of elemen-
tary school because it was feared they might infect fellow
students or teachers. On August 5, 1987, a federal court
ordered the boys' school to reinstate them, but, far from
normalizing the Rays' life, the judgment unleashed a tor-
rent of death threats against the family, culminating in the
August 28, 1987 torching of their home, at which point
the Rays fled to Sarasota. "If the good citizens of Arcadia,
Florida, could chase from their midst an average, law-
abiding family," Bersani wrote, "it is, I would suggest,
because in looking at three hemophiliac children they may
have seen—that is, unconsciously represented—the infinitely more seductive and intolerable image of a grown

man, legs high in the air, unable to refuse the suicidal ecstasy of being a woman."

Larry Kramer had been more blunt on the subject in "1,112 and Counting": "All gays are blamed for John Gacy, the North American Man/Boy Love Association, and AIDS." Maybe this sublimated rage faded over time or maybe we just stopped talking about it, but by the mid-nineties it had been supplanted or supplemented by the entropic psychological effect of what had by then become the standard formula with which people with AIDS were depicted in books and movies and on the news—the "normal" life, the "nagging" cough, the "shocking" diagnosis, the "inexorable" decline—a biographical shorthand as anodyne and irrelevant as Thomas Mulcahy's flowerbeds and Anthony Marrero's Phillies tryout and Michael Sakara's rendition of "I'll Be Seeing You." Just enough information was given to arouse the audience's sympathy, not in an individual but in a human outline who, but for a few details, could have been "you," could have been "me." The only real variable was whether the subject died or lived at story's end, although in either case the experience was, to reclaim a word from Camille Paglia (assuming anyone remembers Camille Paglia), chthonic, and cathartic as well. And as Bertolt Brecht pointed out nearly a century ago (does anyone remember Bertolt Brecht?), the effect of catharsis—indeed, its very goal, as reflected in its original Greek meaning of purgation or purification—is to cleanse the psyche of extremes of emotion, thus rendering it complacent. An empathic connection with a person or perhaps even a situation or cause is first kindled and then expelled (in the case of the AIDS narrative, the sexual overtones of Brecht's metaphor are mordantly resonant), and the resulting psychic lethargy works against moral insight and moral action and in favor of the status quo.

As someone whose first novel had been one of those ever-proliferating AIDS narratives—as someone, more-over, who left ACT UP to devote himself to writing and had unknowingly profited from speculation that he might be HIV-positive—I felt complicit in what I saw as the normalizing of the epidemic into just another hazard of contemporary life. I identified with Kurt Vonnegut when he wrote in *Palm Sunday* of the firebombing of Dresden, which he survived and later chronicled in *Slaughter-house-Five*: "One way or another, I got two or three dollars for every person killed." These words haunted me in the mid-nineties. But unlike my peers, most of whom stopped writing about AIDS around that time (the Lambdas did away with a distinct prize for AIDS writing in 1992, the year before my first novel came out), I couldn't find a way *not* to write about the epi-demic. And though I would have liked to claim that I'd found the right way to write about AIDS, I was far from confident that that was the case, and had to settle for telling myself that I was at least *looking* for the right way. Among other directives, I took to heart a passage from "Is the Rectum a Grave?":

At the very least, such things as the Justice Department's near recommendation that people with AIDS be thrown out of their jobs suggest that if Edwin Meese would not hold a gun to the head of a man with AIDS, he might not find the murder of a gay man with AIDS (or without AIDS?) intolerable or unbearable. And this is precisely what can be said of millions of fine Germans who never participated in the murder of Jews (and of homosexuals), but who *failed to find the idea of the Holocaust unbearable.* That was the more than sufficient measure of their collaboration, the message they sent to their Führer even before the Holocaust began but when the *idea* of it was around, was, as it were, being tested for acceptability during the '30s by less violent but nonetheless virulent manifestations of anti-Semitism.

If I could not achieve the Brechtian ideal—if my emotional investment in the subject would not allow me to abandon the cathartic mode—then I would aim for the Bersanian. I would try to craft a narrative in which the reader could take no consolation in the depictions of AIDS and the people it afflicted, would instead be forced to find the existence of the epidemic unbearable. I'm not sure if I overestimated my ability or underestimated the mental torpor of the bourgeois book-buyer, but in either case neither I nor my audience was able to foresee the development of combination therapy in 1996, and the almost instantaneous transformation of the public conception of AIDS from a death sentence into a manageable chronic illness.

But that was still a year away. In 1995, discussions about AIDS retained the dubious honor of being teleological. All were elaborations of a single fact, and that fact was this: *there was no cure*. Of course, there's still no cure—no cure, no vaccine, no way of getting the drugs we do have to millions of people, both here and in countries that are unable to pay for, distribute, or supervise their use, and no way to tell how long they'll continue to work for the people who do have access to them. In this regard AIDS has become a conversation with a Yeatsian center, which is perhaps the only way people can continue to talk about it without giving in to despair, or murderous rage. But lest we forget: the real—the *only*—solution to the AIDS epidemic will not be imaginative but, rather, scientific and bureaucratic. It will be a cure, and, just as important, the means to get that cure into the bodies of people infected with HIV. But until we have that cure, it is the imagination that must provide us with ways of facing this disease. From the time I started writing I wanted to be a part of this imaginative succor. I thought my first novel was about AIDS, but later came to realize that the hopelessness and grief and search for identity at the core of that book are not so much the hopelessness and grief we feel when confronted by AIDS as much as the hopelessness we feel when we first comprehend the inevitable fact of death—and those two things, death and AIDS, aren't the same thing—not now, in 2013, nor even in the late eighties and early nineties when I was writing *Martin and John*. It wasn't until my book was out in the world, however, and I found myself surprised by some of the things said about it (and me), that I understood I had displaced my feelings about my mother's death onto the epidemic, had done the thing I least wanted to do, which was to strip AIDS of its ontological status and make it a symbol, a metaphor—"a universal story about love and loss and the redemptive powers of fiction," as Michiko Kakutani was kind enough to say in the *Times*. I displaced my anger at myself onto her too, for pointing out what I saw as an artistic and moral failing.

It's a lesson every writer has to learn when he or she crosses the bridge into publication, but I was unprepared for it, which is one of the reasons why I tried my hand at journalism in 1993 and '94 and '95, and also why I pretty much abandoned it after 1996, by which point I had learned that the journalist or memoirist finds it even harder than the novelist to prevent real people and events from being turned—reduced—to symbol. I took Janet Malcolm at face value when she declared, "Every journalist who is not too stupid or too full of himself to notice what is going on knows that what he does is morally indefensible"—but only after I'd published half a dozen fulsome essays and articles of my own. Nonfiction presents a sliver as the whole. It offers the proverbial slice of life, but while the writer's focus is on the slice, the reader's is on life, which, after all, admits neither ellipsis nor abbreviation. Existence is indivisible. It is either whole or it is false. In order to represent it, then, a writer must capitulate to this synecdochal fabrication. Some do so consciously, others blindly, but in either case even the most sophisticated of readers tends to be unaware of or unconcerned with what he considers a problem of classroom aesthetics or navel-gazing postmodernism—until, that is, he sees himself depicted in someone else's words, in which case his reaction is almost always "That's not *me*," which, under interrogation, is usually fine-tuned to "That's not *all* of me." Hence the familiar expressions of outrage from one community or another when it sees a depiction of one of its own that it (or, more accurately, some of its members) dislikes. These depictions are always said to be "not representative," not "the real story" or not "the whole story," and their dissemination to the "general public" is said to be "unfair" or "biased." And they're right, of course, at least as far as bias goes (if only in the most literal sense of the word), though I often think their energy would be better spent educating themselves about how representation works rather than clamoring after the Sisyphean goal of a genuinely mimetic journalism or memoir (by which is usually meant a whitewashed or politically correct version of reality). Because Malcolm's admonition to writers targets only half the problem. The other half is the reader, whose conception of the narrative enterprise tends to be even more unsophisticated than that of the average writer. But then, that's not the reader's problem, is it? It's the writer's.

diverse group this time around, in terms of race and gender and indeed sexual identity, a time when the word "gay" in many organizations' names was replaced (although often only nominally) with "gay and lesbian," then "gay, lesbian, and bisexual," then "gay, lesbian, bisexual, and transgender," then "gay, lesbian, bisexual, transgender, and intersex," an all-inclusive mouthful that was increasingly, in everyday speech if not official communications, replaced with "queer" (or with "gay," although now "gay" was supposed to mean "gay, lesbian, bisexual, transgender, intersex," and whatever new or as-yet undeclared sexual identity might reveal itself next). But no matter what they called themselves, late eighties' queers weren't content with second-class status. Whether they would rattle their cups against the gates of the heterosexual palace and demand, in Bruce Bawer's puling phrase, "a place at the table," or carve out a separate but equal sphere was still up for grabs. For a hot minute, in fact, it looked like the Liberian vision would win out, and I've often wondered where we would have ended up if combination therapy hadn't come along, not to mention the tech boom, which lured both the left and right into throwing over their ideals for the sake of easy money. But if, physically, the improvement was immediately apparent, the cultural gains were measured in smaller increments. In, say, a shift in vocabulary: in 1991, for example, when *Millennium Approaches* premiered and gay men were still railing at newspapers and magazines for not acknowledging the true status of same-sex relationships (c.f., Craig Lucas and

Norman René's *Longtime Companion* or Allen Barnett's
"The *Times* As It Knows Us"), the preferred term for two
men in a longterm relationship was still "lovers." But by the
time *Angels* made it to HBO in 2003 "lover" was giving way
to "husband," which, though tinged with irony, was nevertheless a harbinger of the near-total emphasis on marriage
equality that would take over the gay rights movement
after the war against AIDS had been "won." Then, too,
there was the question of where you used these words,
the government offices or job interviews in which "lover"
or "husband" became "friend" or "roommate" or "that guy
with me," or when you just bit your tongue. In the fifties
and sixties you made the change out of shame, in the seventies and eighties out of fear, in the nineties out of prudence;
but by the time the millennium rolled around you didn't
make it at all, and, what's more, hardly remembered doing
it in the past.

Because freedom, it turned out, wasn't like a new shoe:
you didn't need to break it in. It felt comfortable the first
time you tried it on. It wasn't the present that pinched, but
the past. Brecht, no doubt, wouldn't have approved of this
decidedly ahistoric dialectic, but I think Tony Kushner
might. Kushner hates capitalist imperialism—and, God
bless him, he's one of the few people who can articulately
express this point of view on a national stage—but his
queer politics have, at least since *Angels in America*, been
inclusive to the point of assimilationist. Indeed, they're so
downright domestic it's tempting to call them sentimental,

when in fact they're steeped in an understanding of the human psyche as sophisticated as it is compassionate. I was reminded of this when, in 2003, I watched Mike Nichols's adaptation of *Angels*—and, as well, reminded of how much things had changed in the previous decade, regardless of how far we still had to go. *Angels* is generally considered the most significant literary response to the AIDS epidemic (and justifiably so), yet when I watched it on television a decade after its theatrical premiere it felt strangely flat. Part of the problem is a straightforward conflict of genres: unlike Nichols's earlier adaptation of *Who's Afraid of Virginia Woolf?* (or, for that matter, *The Birdcage*), *Angels* insisted on its theatrical origins after it was filmed. As a play, it's deliberately, powerfully anachronistic in its approach to narrative, updating—one wants to say outing—the mid-century work of Williams and Albee. It's steeped in conversation, soliloquy, a linguistic framing of ideas that's less articulation than excavation, and its characters interact with one another rather than their environment because, as the subtitle reminds us, the play is a fantasia (and a gay one too, with all the cultural as well as sexual associations that word brings). There's something interior and not quite real about it. Onstage, Prior's visions exist within a devolving continuum of what we think of as reality, a dislocation achieved more than anything else by the play's language, which moves from the quotidian to the metaphysical in ever-accelerating cadences, but on the small screen such flights of fancy just look fake.

Technical quibbles aside, though, the real obstacle to the miniseries's success was nostalgia: Kushner's, Nichols's, mine, the nation's. Because W.'s America of 2003, the year of the HBO adaptation, wasn't Bill Clinton's America of 1993, when the play premiered; which was already at an electoral remove from the America of 1991 and 1992 when the play was being written and workshopped and George H.W. Bush was fighting to stay in office; and removed even further from the America of 1985 that the play is set in, when Ronald Reagan had just won a second term by one of the largest electoral margins in history. At any rate it wasn't the same America for gay people. History had been accelerated for us during the previous two decades. Civil rights battles that might have taken generations took only a few years, sometimes a few months; and though those battles were (and are) far from over, it's safe to say that in 2003 gay men occupied a demonstrably more secure position than we did in 1992, or 1985. When Joe says to Louis, "Look, I want to touch you. Can I just touch you here?" he means both on the cheek, and also in Central Park—in public. For the hundredth, the thousandth time, a gay man was coming out to America, and it seemed perhaps that this time it took. We were safer in 2003, more visible, more capable of influencing the things said about us on a national level, and we owed that power to *Angels in America* and the intense cultural and political project of which it had been a part—but we were not, as was, I think, Kushner's hope (not to mention his audience's), capable of influencing the things America said about itself. History had acknowledged us, but it had also passed us by, by which I mean that the cultural and political response to AIDS made gay men more American, but it didn't make Americans more gay. Whether you regard capitalism as selfish or selfless, inspiring or greedy, an exporter of democratic values or an exploiter of the inhabitants and resources of the third world, the thing that will save the planet or the thing that will destroy it, the marketplace has proven remarkably flexible in assimilating gay male notions of masquerade, subterfuge, and subversion without itself being subverted by them. By which I mean that when I watched *Angels* in 1992 and 1993 I knew who I was: I knew who the play thought I was, and the play was right. But in 2003 I didn't feel like the play was talking to me anymore. I didn't feel like it knew who I was, because I didn't feel like *I* knew who I was, not as a gay man anyway, nor as someone who had lived through the pre–combination therapy years of the AIDS epidemic, which existed in memory with the unreal quality of a military occupation. As the distantly familiar scenes flashed by on my TV, I felt like I was watching a home movie that had been shot when I was just barely old enough to remember—a movie in which I was, moreover, speaking French or Spanish or some other language I not only no longer understood, but didn't remember ever knowing, and, if I can unite the two metaphors—war, language—I couldn't help but wonder if the language I spoke now was my own, or a kind of colonial imposition. By which I mean that George Bush was president when Tony Kushner first wrote *Angels*, and George Bush was president when it was turned into a miniseries ten years later. By which I mean that perhaps it wasn't the miniseries that didn't do the play justice, it was the times. By which I mean, finally, that as soon as I finished watching *Angels* the only thing I could think to do was watch it again, because I wanted it to have a second chance.

IT WAS TONY Kushner who, in 1995, let me know that Leo Bersani's *Homos* had been published, and it was *Homos* that made me realize I was on Kushner's side—on the side of, if not domesticity, then human lives that resembled (with apologies to Herr Goethe) the elective affinities with which I was familiar, as opposed to performative modalities that often seemed like experiments in egotism and anomie. Queer theory, I realized when I read *Homos* in April of 1995, and the seven- or eight-year activist idyll it had helped usher into being, had run its course as a popular (populist?) intellectual force: whatever would happen next would happen somewhere else, in some other way. I don't mean to say that *Homos* killed queer theory, let alone queer activism, only that, in the very audacity with which it invited readers "to rethink what we mean and what we expect from communication, and from community," Bersani's own arguments made the practical limitations of queer theory plain to me, particularly as it applied to the AIDS epidemic. No, that's not quite it either. One of the great attractions of queer theory was its extraordinary reach across genres and disciplines, indeed across time, as it shined new light on the past and revealed the way in which sex, sexuality, and gender, far from being the rigid entailments that our neo-Victorian sensibilities had been schooled to think of as naturally and morally immutable, have in fact been in flux for as long as stories have been told. From that reimaged past, queer theory offered up at the very least the *possibility* of new ways of being in the not-too-distant future—the future that was in some apparent or implied way under construction at every ACT UP and Queer Nation demo, every community forum such as "Talk Sex" and the one sponsored by Gay and Lesbian HIV Prevention Activists, every academic and artistic conference devoted to queer arts and letters. "The soul is the prison of the body," Foucault told us in *Discipline and Punish*, and it had been the privilege of philosophers and artists since time immemorial to contemplate the nature of that cage: whether it was of divine or mundane origin; what could and couldn't be accomplished within its confines; if there was any means of escape. But AIDS was a cell inside the body inside the prison—an internal ankle monitor, as it were, as opposed to stone and bars and razor wire—and until a cure or vaccine was invented it would forever inhabit and inhibit the range and variety of the body's actions, and, hence, of the moral imagination.

There comes a moment in almost every individual's life when he believes, rightly or wrongly, that *he can be whatever he wants*, but for queers in the late eighties and early nineties that prospect was infinitely more exciting, because we felt *we could make the world into what we wanted it to be*. And it was this sense of near-infinite possibility that *Homos* made me realize had been prematurely and permanently derailed by the AIDS epidemic. It was at one of the conferences mentioned above—at OutWrite, a colloquium on queer writing held each spring in Boston from 1989 to 1999—that Tony Kushner, in his opening plenary address, brought the long-awaited follow-up to "Is the Rectum a Grave?" to my attention. "Professor Bersani has published a new book called *Homos*," Kushner told a rapt audience of several hundred. "Let me read you a paragraph found on page sixty-nine":

> To move to an entirely different register, Tony Kushner's *Angels in America* has analogous ambitions. For Kushner, to be gay in the 1980s was to be a metaphor not only for Reagan's America but for the entire history of America, a country in which there are "no gods . . . no ghosts and spirits . . . no angels . . . no spiritual past, no racial past, there's only the political." The enormous success of this muddled and pretentious play is a sign, if we need still another one, of how ready and anxious America is to see and hear about gays—provided we reassure America how familiar, how morally sincere, and, particularly in the case of Kushner's work, how innocuously full of significance we can be.

I want to enter *Homos* through this passage. In context, it's nothing more than a snide aside, 120 words trivializing a seven-hour play and the enormous cultural response it engendered. It appears a third of the way into what had seemed until then a coherent, persuasive argument, but as I read the rest of *Homos* the shrillness of this particular passage—and the denial that shrillness usually masks—became revelatory to me.

Tellingly, *Homos*'s last reference to AIDS occurs in the early pages of the third of its four longish chapters: "Having always longed to be one of those happy gays myself," Bersani wrote, "I can't help wondering what the pleasures were that led to this enviable absence of any interpretive aftertaste in the men Foucault probably did see, less frequently, I would guess, in Paris than around Castro Street where he lived when, during the glorious pre-AIDS years of the late 1970s, he was a visiting professor at Berkeley." Hiding inside this somewhat convoluted sentence was the evocation of "the glorious pre-AIDS years," and it was there that Bersani's consciousness seemed to remain for the rest of his book, as *Homos* redirected its attention to, you might say, "the glorious pre-AIDS years" of the first half of the twentieth century. In its first two chapters *Homos* had picked up where "Is the Rectum a Grave?" left off in 1987, arguing what had by 1995 become a virtual truism (in large part because of arguments made by Bersani, Simon Watney, and the people who wrote in their wake), namely, that "nothing has made gay men more visible than AIDS," and that "homophobic virulence in America has increased in direct proportion to the wider acceptance of homosexuals." But where other writers might simply have argued for queers to redouble their efforts in the battle for equal rights and against HIV, Bersani made a surprising left turn in *Homos*, declaring: "Never before in the history of minority groups struggling for recognition and equal treatment has there been an analogous attempt, on the part of any such group, to make itself unidentifiable even as it demands to be recognized."

It wasn't a popular assessment then, and it's not a popular assessment now (although the passage of time has, for better and worse, borne it out). But whether or not the political expediency of an innate gay identity will ever be justified by scientific fact, queers will always be defined (at least from the outside) not by their sexual desire but by *whether and how they act on it*. It's sex that makes you gay, at least in the eyes of the straight world, and it's gay sex that made gay culture, not the other way around. In Bersani's view, queers had yet to tap the revolutionary potential of gay sex, a potential rooted in sexual acts that were as free from the trappings of "heteroized sociality" as possible. It should come as no surprise, then, that Bersani was interested in promiscuity. In a footnote to "Is the Rectum a Grave?" he had this to say about Randy Shilts's *And the Band Played On*:

> I won't go into . . . the phenomenon of Shilts himself
> as an overnight media star, and the relation between

his stardom and his irreproachably respectable image, his long-standing willingness, indeed eagerness, to join the straights in being morally repelled by gay promiscuity. A good deal of his much admired "objectivity" as a reporter consists in his being as venomous toward those at an exceptionally high risk of becoming afflicted with AIDS (gay men) as toward the government officials who seem content to let them die.

Bersani's 1987 criticisms seemed apropos to the situation regarding New York's sex clubs in 1995, and, in fact, were still on his mind. From *Homos*: "Recent objections in the gay press to a new bathhouse in San Francisco sounded like Randy Shilts all over again." In fact, one of the strongest elements of *Homos* was its attack on things that promote a "denial of sex"—both sex acts themselves, but also, and more important, the context in which those sex acts occur, and the new contexts they might make possible, viz. this approving, if not simply wistful, quotation from Foucault with which Bersani opened his third chapter: "I think that what most bothers those who are not gay about gayness is the gay life-style, not sex acts themselves . . . It is the prospect that gays will create as yet unforeseen kinds of relationships that many people cannot tolerate."

It's tempting to say that AIDS hijacked the Foucauldian inquiry into these "as yet unforeseen kinds of relationships," not least because the disease claimed Foucault's life in

1984, but also because the epidemic consumed almost the entirety of gay political and cultural activity for a decade and a half, during which time the words "gay" and "AIDS" became inextricably linked as cultural signifiers, and almost any gay political campaign was seen as an extension of the fight against AIDS, and any effort to combat the epidemic as advancing the "homosexual agenda." Foucault's claim seems less tenable in hindsight, given that, in the wake of the so-called "end of AIDS" in 1996, the gay agenda moved rapidly to the center (about which, said the happily married homosexual, *sigh*), but it's important to remember that in 1995 the future looked far from certain, and Bersani's inquiry into the kinds of new relationships gays, and gay sex, might produce seemed neither academic nor esoteric. Okay, it seemed *both* academic and esoteric, but it also seemed like the kind of question that could be asked only by someone who considered himself a member of a group that felt itself to be at a profound threshold—a group that could be seen as occupying territory analogous to that of freed slaves in the wake of the Civil War or of various Eastern European peoples after the collapse of the Soviet Union in 1991, or perhaps simply of any emigrant who leaves behind the old country, the old language, the old culture, for a new one. In the wake of the visibility that AIDS had thrust on queers, and that ACT UP and queer theory had helped to solidify into genuine, if qualified, political power, queers were asking themselves who they wanted to be now, not just as individuals, but as a the very impossibility of being a good citizen, assuming we capitulate to a Gidean model of what Bersani called "intimacies devoid of intimacy." In Proust's *Sodom and Gomorrah*, with its extensive and uncritical exploration of the idea that male homosexuality is the condition of a woman's soul trapped in a man's body, Bersani found a "dance of essences" in which "the multiplication and crisscrossing of gender identifications ... defeats any cultural securities about what it might mean to be a man or a woman." And finally, in Genet's *Funeral Rites*, Bersani saw proof of the view of history that believes (pessimistically, if not simply conservatively) that any overtly political move replicates the institutions of power it seeks to overthrow with identically "oppressive conditions." The evidence, then (selective as even Bersani admitted it was), seemed to argue in favor of the "revolutionary inaptitude" of homosexual desire for "heteroized sociality" that Bersani talked about back in 1987, although this came across not as tautological but as a kind of making good on an earlier bluff: Bersani had laid his aces on the table. But what prize was he claiming?

Taken collectively, Gide, Proust, and Genet's novels formed the core of a canon that, in Bersani's reading, offered glimpses of an escape from the tyranny of "the self," which Bersani saw as "the precondition for registration and service as a citizen." "Personhood," Bersani told readers, is "a status that the law needs in order to discipline us and, it must be added, to protect us." This self or personhood seems to bear the same relationship to consciousness as the puppet does to its invisible master—save that, in Bersani's model, the puppet has the real power, by limiting the master's expressions and actions to those he can transmit through his wires to the puppet's facsimile of a body. Ostensibly nothing more than a middleman between society and the unquantifiable array of cognitive processes it was created to represent—i.e., consciousness, for lack of a more specific term—the self, like a modern multinational bank, has grown so large that its own concerns have come to dominate both the internal and external realities it mediates. Hence all psychic and social activity will ultimately be in its service rather than a community's—selfish, in the simplest locution, rather than selfless. (And yes, I'm aware I switched from a fairly extended conceit about puppets to a second one about banking in the middle of that explanation: such are the prerogatives of the self, which cares not a whit for Aristotelian aesthetic unities.)

In his 1990 book *The Culture of Redemption*, Bersani rejected the idea of art's redemptive power based on a Freudian notion of the origins of art, arguing that art should not be used to redeem the things of the real world for the simple reason that it cannot. Bersani's notion of homosexuality, though "problematized," as we said so often in the eighties and nineties, was equally, indeed resolutely, Freudian. For Bersani, homosexual desire is a turning away from the other toward the same, and an identity based on this turning-away must, by rights, be equally asocial. "Art perhaps knows nothing but such confused beginnings," Bersani wrote with Ulysse Dutoit in *Arts of Impoverishment*, "and in pushing us back to them it beneficently mocks the accumulated wisdom of culture." But as Tony Kushner pointed out in his opening address at OutWrite, in order to mock the accumulated wisdom of culture you must first be part of it. These tensions—between the desires to destroy and to create, between the explicit desire to be asocial and the implicit recognition that any work of art is inevitably social—produced the occasional shrill note in *Homos*, such as his pan of *Angels in America*, and these shrill notes, as I said, became revelatory to me, particularly the last and most significant of them, when Bersani asked his readers to contemplate Genet's love of Nazism as a model for their own behavior. (Yes, you read that correctly.) In Genet's Nazi worship, Bersani saw "an unqualified will to destroy" that created "a myth of absolute betrayal—the betrayal of all human ties," and he arrived at this conclusion through an exegesis that must be experienced to be appreciated:

> This is not a political program. Just as Genet's fascination with what he outrageously calls the beauty of Nazism is in no way a plea for the specific goals pursued by Nazi Germany, Erik and Riton are positioned for a reinventing of the social without any indication about how such a reinvention might proceed historically or what face it might have. *Funeral Rites* does nothing more—but I think it's a great deal—than propose the fantasmatic

conditions of possibility for such a proceeding. It insists on the continuity between the sexual and the political, and while this superficially glorifies Nazism as the system most congenial to a cult of male power justified by little more than male beauty, it also transforms the historical reality of Nazism into a mythic metaphor for a revolutionary destructiveness which would surely dissolve the rigidly defined sociality of Nazism itself. Still, the metaphoric suitability of Hitler's regime for this project can hardly be untroubling. It reminds us only too clearly that Genet's political radicalism is congruent with a proclaimed indifference to human life as well as a willingness to betray every tie and every trust between human beings. This is the evil that becomes Genet's good, and, as if that were not sufficiently noxious, homosexuality is enlisted as the prototype of relations that break with humanity, that elevate infecundity, waste, and sameness to requirements for the production of pleasures. ¶ There may be only one reason to tolerate, even to welcome, *Funeral Rites*'s rejection (at once exasperated and clownish) of relationality: without such a rejection, social revolt is doomed to repeat the oppressive conditions that provoked the revolt.

If you separated Bersani's message from its "mythic metaphor"—which, while perfectly acceptable within at the expense of *every person living with HIV* and *every person who might become infected* before our old selves, both as individuals and as a culture, had been destroyed and remade, and possibly even after. It takes institutions to fight an epidemic: medical, scientific, above all political, but it was precisely these kinds of bureaucracies that Bersani's "revolutionary" program sought to destroy. And what would a world in which "relationality" has been "rejected" look like? None of the authors Bersani cited gives us any real idea what to look (let alone work) for: "*The Immoralist*," Bersani admitted, "has nothing to tell us about such a society," and, similarly, *Funeral Rites* offers no "indication about how such a reinvention might proceed historically or what face it might have." Proust "does sketch the outlines of a community grounded in a desire indifferent to the established sanctity of personhood," but all Bersani told readers about this "community" was that "the person disappears in his or her desire, a desire that seeks more of the same, partially dissolving subjects by extending them into a communal homo-ness." In other words, Proust doesn't tell us much either. It's tempting to say that what this world most looks like is a gay sex club, but if that's the case then it's a club along the lines of Gabriel Rotello's "AIDS killing grounds" rather than a haven of "brotherly" love. But even the idea of an institution in which all this self-destroying sex can take place would have botched the experiment—would, as such clubs did in 1975 and 1985 and 1995, albeit in very different ways in each of these signal moments, provide a psychologically safe space in which the flesh is mortified even as the psyche is given a respite from the relentless homophobia that exists beyond the clubs' doors. In fact it seemed that what you really needed was a place like 924 N. 25th St., #213, Milwaukee, Wisconsin 53233, i.e., the apartment of Jeffrey Dahmer, in which twelve gay men found their personhood "partially dissolved" in a vat of acid before Dahmer flushed them down the toilet.

Is this—to use one of Bersani's favorite words to describe an argument he considers to have been pushed to a kitschy extreme—"bitchy"? Probably. But how was one supposed to respond rationally to a call for queers to cease caring for one another as a first step toward a utopian project that the author himself couldn't or wouldn't describe? This was 1995, remember: a year in which 50,000 Americans died from AIDS and 200,000 more were trying not to. A year in which AIDS activism had run of out of ideas, AIDS fatigue had become entrenched in queer life, and AIDS research appeared from the outside to be at a standstill. And, for me, it was also the year in which I came to understand how completely AIDS circumscribed the body, not just as a material entity, but an imagined one. It was in 1995 that I finally realized that to write about sex without mentioning AIDS was merely that: to write about sex without mentioning AIDS. AIDS was still there; it was merely unsaid. To set a work of fiction in some pre- or post-AIDS utopia was as much a comment on AIDS's stifling power as anything else, and the same held true for a work of nonfiction that derived its ethos from "the glorious pre-AIDS years" of the

One wants at the very least to be able to write about AIDS as Kurt Vonnegut wrote about the bombing of Dresden in *Slaughterhouse-Five*: "It begins like this: *Listen*," and "It ends like this: *Poo-tee-weet?*" But we don't have our befuddled anthropomorphized bird, confused by the things humans do. We don't have the words "It ends." Our bombs have not yet stopped falling.

As it turned out I was wrong about that too—at least according to Andrew Sullivan, who, in an essay entitled "When Plagues End," which appeared in the Nov. 10, 1996 issue of the *New York Times Magazine*, proclaimed "the end of AIDS," and dismissed with beneficent condescension those who "find it hard to accept that this ordeal *as a whole* may be over" (my intentionally cunty italics). For Sullivan, AIDS was—pardon me, *had been*—a gay plague, "a quintessentially homosexual experience," and though he acknowledged that "the vast majority of HIV-positive people in the world, and a significant minority in America, will not have access to the expensive and effective new drug treatments," their suffering was, *as a whole*, of a different order to that of the gay friends whose capsule biographies punctuate his essay. AIDS, Sullivan informed us, had been "a natural calamity, singling out a group of despised outsiders by virtue of a freak of nature" rather than a straightforward viral epidemic whose appearance in the gay community had been foreshadowed in the outbreaks of a plethora of STDs throughout the 1970s, and whose initial impact was

magnified a thousandfold by the homophobically moti-
vated disregard of the government, media, medical
establishment, and general population. Of the pre-AIDS,
pre–safe sex lifestyle that served, quite literally, as the
breeding grounds for disease, Sullivan seemed only
obliquely and then disparagingly conscious: "Responsibility," he wrote, is not a word "one usually associated with
homosexuality":

> Before AIDS, gay life—rightly or wrongly—was iden-
> tified with freedom from responsibility, rather than
> with its opposite. Gay liberation was most commonly
> understood as liberation from the constraints of tra-
> ditional norms, almost a dispensation that permitted
> homosexuals the absence of responsibility in return
> for an acquiescence in second-class citizenship. This
> was the Faustian bargain of the pre-AIDS closet:
> straights gave homosexuals a certain amount of free-
> dom; in return, homosexuals gave away their
> self-respect.

"Freedom from responsibility" in a world in which one's
sexuality was illegal and one's right to assemble and express
oneself was routinely denied? "Liberation from the constraints
of traditional norms" when exposure as a homosexual could
mean the loss of one's job, one's home, one's liberty, one's life?
"Homosexuals gave away their self-respect" because they
found a way to have fun (and sex) in a manner that wasn't

sanctified by a revisionist interpretation of Judeo-Christian norms? Even in 1996, Sullivan's version of gay history seemed based almost entirely on the "murderous representations of homosexuals unleashed and 'legitimized' by AIDS" that Leo Bersani had deplored nine years earlier—based not on the events of the previous fifteen years, but on the "stigma and the guilt and the fear" Sullivan told readers he felt about being gay, and the "shame" he felt at having contracted HIV. In sharp contrast to the writers Bersani accused of idealizing pre-AIDS gay life, Sullivan swung the opposite direction, demonizing it as a nonstop party that, in the wake of combination therapy, he saw being "repeated as farce" in the form of circuit parties and "as tragedy" in the form of sex clubs. Thus the reason that "many of us find it hard to accept that this ordeal as a whole may be over" was because "we may now be required to relent from our clenching against the future and remember—and give meaning to—the past."

This analysis of the "psychological roots" of gay men's response to the advent of combination therapy said in essence that the first fifteen years of the AIDS epidemic had no "meaning" other than what might retroactively be ascribed to it, and went on to tell readers that giving "meaning" to the past is merely a question of representing it with the future in mind—or rather *a* future, the one that Sullivan was attempting to conjure into being with his words. Here, then, was the right way to write about AIDS—not by bucking the trend of familiarization, but by accelerating it. Not by urging readers to work for the end of the epidemic, but by informing them that—thanks to their efforts!—it was already over. In Sullivan's revision of the American plague, TAG is a group whose only quality is its "skepticism," while ACT UP is nothing more than a "dark, memorable flash of activism" born of "decades of euphemism and self-loathing." The "end of AIDS" had been initiated not by these AIDS activists but, rather, by America (and by "America" Sullivan clearly doesn't mean its queer citizenry): "America might have responded the way many Latin American and Asian countries responded," Sullivan wrote of the nation whose president didn't mention the epidemic in public until Sept. 17, 1985, whose acting press secretary regularly chuckled when asked about AIDS, and whose executive branch, in 1987, banned HIV-positive people from entering its borders (which prohibition Sullivan lived in violation of until Barack Obama repealed it on October 30, 2009): "with almost complete silence and denial." But perhaps the most startling thing about the "meaning" Sullivan ascribed to the (now vanquished) epidemic was the magnification of the gay plague in America—which by the time Sullivan wrote had already been revealed as a footnote to a global catastrophe—into the central fact of the epidemic, whereas the "vast majority of HIV-positive people in the world" were mere statistical phenomena, lives and deaths to whom was denied the redemptive, revisionist "meaning" with which Sullivan privileged his own experience.

In his 1994 review of *Schindler's List*, J. Hoberman wrote: "Leave it to Steven Spielberg to make a feel-good movie entertainment about the ultimate feel-bad experience." Sullivan achieves what I would have thought was a similarly impossible feat in "When Plagues End," somehow making me *resent* the quote-privileged-unquote status of the western gay man with AIDS, and the ownership some gay men took of the epidemic—without which the "expensive and effective new drug treatments" that, eighteen years later, still remain out of reach for "the vast majority of HIV-positive people in the world, and a significant minority in America," would likely not have existed until many years after they did. In 1990, in *The Body and Its Dangers*—the only book he lived to write—Allen Barnett surmised that the world would be divided into "HIVs" and "HIV-nots." It turns out, however, that the camps are, as they've always been, the haves and have-nots: almost two decades after Sullivan made the case that the life of a gay American man (or gay Brit living in America) is worth more than the life of a straight African, or straight African-American for that matter, the western world seems to have acquiesced to his view of the situation. About which one more quote: "The record of humanity is a record of sorrows." This is the hapless cuckold John Dowell in *The Good Soldier*, whose maxim is given in willful ignorance of another truism about history, namely, that it's written by the victors, whose privilege it is to give "meaning" to the past—to, in the final analysis, decide when the past is indeed passed. If the bombs won't stop falling, change the channel on the war.

13

November 12, 1996

Dale Peck
92 St. Mark's Place, #4
New York, NY 10009
tel: (212) 388-0461
fax: (212) 254-5717

Letters to the Editor
Magazine
The New York Times
229 W. 43rd Street
New York, NY 10036

To the Editor:

It is understandable that Andrew Sullivan, as a P.W.A., should invest a great amount of hope in protease inhibitors; but, as a journalist, he should have known better than to forecast the end of the AIDS pandemic based on a treatment regimen that, in the first place, does not work for everyone who tries it, in the second, is not available to the vast majority of people with H.I.V. and AIDS, and, in the third, has only been in serious testing for one year. That protease inhibitors have had profoundly beneficial effects for many

P.W.A.s is cause for celebration and perhaps even for hope; nevertheless, an enormous amount of research still needs to be done on these and many other drugs, and a prediction of victory in the battle against AIDS—let alone victory itself—is still years away. Mr. Sullivan has cottoned on to a mood among certain persons involved in the pandemic and distorted it into a manifesto that is in reality not much more than a wish-fulfillment fantasy. And, while I pray that Mr. Sullivan is in fact correct in his predictions, prudence—and, more to the point, an attentiveness to scientific fact—would have served better than the three or four mini-biographies of P.W.A.s he offers instead. Empathy probably won't hurt anyone struggling with this disease, but it won't help them much either, and it won't cure anyone.

Dale Peck

14

I was a foot soldier in an army small enough that the generals and the grunts were in daily contact with each other—at its peak, there were perhaps a thousand people at ACT UP's Monday night meetings, and only one or two actions a year managed to get even half that many people on the streets. I'd say I was the equivalent of cannon fodder,

but that'd push the metaphor into an uncomfortable place—
the truth is I had a better chance of surviving this war than
far too many of my peers. Like a centurion quaking when
Caesar inspected the ranks, I stammered in the presence of
Larry Kramer—the only man I have ever known whom I
consider a hero—and felt blessed, anointed even, when he
deigned to know my name. I make no claims for my time in
ACT UP (or Queer Nation, or Pink Panthers, or WHAM!, or
any of the other offshoots and unofficially affiliated groups
that sprang up in the early nineties). I wasn't a founder or
a leader. I had no ideas, did no heavy lifting, acquired no
specialized knowledge, took no extreme risks, committed
no felonies in the name of civil disobedience (I was arrested
three times, spent perhaps twelve hours total in jail, another
couple in court; in all three instances I received an ACD, or
adjournment in contemplation of dismissal, which is the
judicial equivalent of a slap on the wrist, except there's no
slap). All I did was give thirty or so hours of my time each
week: in meetings and marches; at actions and demos;
working phone trees; xeroxing and stapling flyers; assem-
bling bleach kits for addicts to clean their works and
exchanging new needles for used ones; patrolling the
streets of the West Village to deter gaybashers. And I educated myself: for three or four years I read almost nothing
that hadn't been published in the previous decade or been
written by a gay man or lesbian or bisexual or transgen-
dered person—everything else lacked urgency to me,
seemed so divorced from the present moment as to lack all

leaders—then blame the Wright brothers (but please, *please* don't blame Gaëtan Dugas). I do think, though, that the (perhaps necessary) naiveté that informed the sexual revolution profoundly deepened the psychic impact of AIDS. A quarter of the population of Europe died from bubonic plague, after all, but by and large the population's faith in its traditional institutions wasn't shaken, because rats had never been one of those institutions. But Americans, straight as well as gay, had chosen to believe in sex: we'd decided, in fact, that it would save us. In a world that seemed to lack both god and benevolent politicians, we'd reclaimed a concept of Dionysian excess, christened it free love, and declared it humanity's last hope. But before the bacchanal could save anybody—or fail to save anybody—it emerged that it was in fact killing us, and we were left with an enormous cultural experiment that had not been disproved as much it had been destroyed. Our prophets held up their books and icons, but the words had been erased now, the images rendered invisible. In the space of a few years the sexual revolution dissolved like the wetted Wicked Witch of the West: it caved in on itself, an empty dress collapsing in on its bodiless core, and the soldiers who had once fought in its service rushed to stamp on its remains.

So: yes. A bad time. But when youth syncs up with such epochal moments, a tone is set. The sexual revolution belonged to my parents' generation, after all, and the first great wave of AIDS deaths affected a similarly aged population. I lost an opportunity, a context, but I didn't lose the hundreds or thousands of friends that people a decade or two older than me did. And I got to be present at the birth of something new. Something that permanently changed the position of queers in American society, and less palpably but no less importantly, the way that society thought about sexuality and sexual identity. Compared to that, the information revolution seems to me a paltry thing, a mechanistic acceleration rather than a genuine change in the way people conceive of and live in the world. What I mean is, I recognize today's teenage straight kids, who resemble the teenage straight kids of my generation, albeit in modern drag, but I don't recognize many of today's teenage gay kids, who have ways of being that didn't exist or weren't possible when I was their age. And you know what? That makes me feel great. Middle-aged, but great. Then, too, there was the fact that in addition to sex we (and again I mean not just queers but all Americans) had chosen to believe in an idea of statehood in which a government is beholden to its people. Notwithstanding conservative bluster about getting government out of the way, the same technological and demographic realities that made possible the global spread of HIV make necessary the intercession of regional bureaucracies on the part of the people they represent, and AIDS activists took the United States and a few European governments to heel for failing in their duties and shamed them into addressing the epidemic. If there was any way in which the first fifteen years of the western gay plague was the global phenomenon that Andrew Sullivan seemed to think then, surprisingly, he asked if I'd heard of a news report the Canadian Broadcasting Company was making about artists and AIDS. I was surprised by this question, to say the least, because I was going to be interviewed for the report the very next day. I asked Gordon how he could have possibly known about it and was even more surprised when he told me that he'd been interviewed for it right before he came to New York. There were, I think, six artists filmed for this story, scattered across Canada and America. The chances that Gordon and I would meet while he was in New York on a weeklong vacation were astronomically low; the chance that the meeting would fall between our interviews made our hookup feel like kismet. That, plus Gordon's obvious intelligence (not to mention the hour-long blowjob he gave me the following day before my interview), were enough to inaugurate a three-year epistolary friendship that produced the most remarkable correspondence of my life.

Another city, another sex club (actually about a year or so before my encounter with Gordon): I met Anthony and Sammy in San Francisco. The circumstances were charged to begin with: I'd run into Derek (of green mohawk fame) at Tunnel Bar in the East Village, and while Derek played pinball he told me how David had dumped him, leaving him with an extra ticket to San Francisco that, before his game was over, he offered to me. On our first or second night in SF I hooked up with Anthony in what I think had been the living room of a Victorian row house that had been

turned into a sex club. As with Gordon, it wasn't a typical
encounter: Anthony was, as the Psych Furs sang, into me
like a train, and soon enough I forgot we were in public—
was surprised, when we finished, to look up and see half
a dozen men surrounding us, jerking off as though we
were putting on a show for their benefit. I needed that,
Anthony said, it's been two months since I had sex. Why?
I asked, and Anthony leaned in and whispered something
I didn't hear. I asked him to repeat himself and he grinned
sheepishly. I had to wait until the last zoster dried up, he
said, louder, and after a moment I shrugged and asked him
to invite me home. He had a boyfriend, Sammy. They didn't
live together, but Sammy called the following morning,
and I had the amusing experience of listening while
Anthony described what we'd done in the club and in his
bed, at the end of which he said, Sammy wants to meet
you. It turned out that Anthony was nervous about getting
fucked by Sammy, who was HIV-positive, and since I'd
decided as soon as I met Sammy that I was going to be the
filling in that sandwich, I happily demonstrated my belief
in safe sex (although I was probably lazier than usual,
since I was already stuffed with the delicious plantain
soufflé Sammy had made for dinner). The next morning
we woke to the news of Jeffrey Dahmer's arrest, the glee-
ful detailing of the body parts in the refrigerator and the
vat of acid beside the bed, and the day I got back to New
York I found a message on my answering machine—
between a message from a telemarketer and another

message from a friend of my roommate's telling her that his boyfriend had died of AIDS—informing me that Farrar Straus and Giroux had made an offer on my first novel, even though my agent had pulled it out of submission more than two months earlier. With all that context, I'm sure I would've remembered the encounter anyway, but Anthony and Sammy moved to New York a year or two later, looked me up, let me know that my ease in bed had made Anthony more confident in the efficacy of condoms, and twenty-two years later they're still together.

But above all I remember Derek Link. Of all the things I could tell you about him, the most relevant is that he was the first person I slept with who told me he was HIV-positive. He told me the night after we met, which is to say, the night after we had sex for the first time. That had been a Thursday, and I decided to skip work on Friday to hang out with him. We went out for breakfast at the old Odessa (I had French toast, he had pancakes). He said he had something to tell me and even as I guessed from his tone what it was he said: "I'm positive." I use quotation marks here because I know these were his actual words: I recorded them on a piece of yellow paper ripped from a legal pad that I later tucked into a new journal. I was a sporadic journaler at best, usually starting one when I felt that something momentous had happened, and I knew that something momentous had happened here. Not that I had slept with an HIV-positive person, but that I had met someone great. Someone about whom I need manufacture none of my usual illusions to love. I already knew from ACT UP that Derek was a member of the inner circle of Treatment and Data, and that alone would have elevated him into an exalted position in my estimation. But it was what he had done before joining ACT UP that cemented my feelings for him. Or, rather, what had been done to him, because Derek, like me, had been a witness, a cog in a brutal adult machine, but unlike me he had not escaped unscathed—he had been gnashed and ground and all but chewed up in the machine's gears. So great was the psychic torment inflicted on him, and so complete was my identification with him, that ten days after I met him I wrote in my new journal: "I know that I will write about us." We only hooked up for a few weeks but months later I was still writing, not because I was carrying the torch but because I was convinced that Derek was "a more authentic version of myself."

From that same journal, in an entry dated January 20, 1991:

I haven't been really writing down what I know about Derek. I've concentrated instead on how I feel about him, and trusted that the mundane facts will remain in my memory. I feel a little guilty just contemplating reducing Derek to a list of historical facts that would begin: b. May 30, 1967; and therefore suggest the ending: d. _____, and I don't really want to think about how soon that date may come. But, for the record:

DEREK LINK

- b. May 30, 1967
- HIV diagnosis: sometime in the summer of '89, since he found out 2 months after graduating college when his best friend/sometime (or one-time) lover, Stephen, was diagnosed with PCP.
- Education: 7 years in English boarding school (11–18); 2 ½ @ Columbia, finishing up at Bard. BA in, I think, Art.
- Sex: Btw. 450–500 men. For the last 2 years, 50 men a year. Before that, 100. Likes bathhouses. Loves getting fucked, having cum on his face/in his mouth. Tells of groups of 8 or so boarding school kids taking turns tying one another to a wire box-springs and gang-banging the victim. Sexually active since 14. Out since 16.
- Before AIDS: Painting was his passion. I've never seen one. He doesn't have space or time for it now. Sculpture, though, and architecture, are his 2 favorite art forms, though he doesn't practice them, because they are 3-D, and therefore a tangible, unavoidable part of reality. He also played in an all–gay boy hardcore band (w/ Stephen).
- He was bashed in Boston in '89. He could've died; his lungs filled up with blood. 4 boys beat him with sticks. None saw jail. He was awarded $20,000 in damages to be paid in installments.

> *The 1st is 2 months late.*
>
> • *Some work: He gave private art lessons to rich kids. $65/hour, ten kids a week. Also painted their portraits: $5,000 a pop. A lot of this money paid for Stephen's health care. He's got plenty in the bank too.*
>
> • *Family: Jewish (changed name from Linkowitz). Father's side has big $. Great-uncle converted to Catholicism and endowed the George Link Pavilion in St. Vincent's. Dad sits on the board of some big company.*

His mother, he told me the second day we were together, had been a Holocaust refugee, fleeing Germany as a little girl and taking up residence in England. She moved to the States, married Derek's father, who was a businessman based in Chicago, while Mrs. Link taught French at Tulane. It was a stuffy family dynamic. Derek was mostly raised by nannies and only saw his mother an hour a day, right before bedtime—from an early age she insisted he only speak to her in French so that he would learn the language. His father came to New Orleans on the weekends, and the family had at least one formal meal together, served by the maid. Derek recounted his week during soup or salad, his mother during the main course, his father during dessert and coffee (to this day, Derek told me, the sight of a waiter approaching the table to clear makes him talk faster). Boarding school in England seemed like an idyll at first, *Lord of the Flies* meets the video for "Total Eclipse of the Heart," but at fifteen or sixteen or maybe seventeen Derek had what was in effect a nervous breakdown, and eventually refused to leave his room. The school contacted his parents but they refused to come get their son, and after it became clear that they weren't bluffing the school had no choice but to put Derek in a mental institution, where, doped up on Thorazine, he lingered for nine months. Eventually Derek's maternal grandmother, who still lived in England, took him in, but Derek ran away and soon enough was hustling on the streets of London, which is probably when he was infected. After a year and a half of this he sent a set of faked O levels? A levels? to Columbia University and, when he was admitted, guilted his parents into paying for it. He did two and a half years at Columbia, then transferred to Bard, where he began hustling again, and after he graduated he moved to Boston to pursue a painting career. He'd had two solo shows and one group exhibition, or one solo show and two group exhibitions, and played in a punk band with three other gay boys, all of whom were fucking one another without condoms, when one of them, Stephen, was admitted to the hospital with PCP. The other members of the band got tested, which is when Derek found out he was positive. After Stephen got out of the hospital, Derek took him to the gay bars in the South End, and on their way home they were bashed by the group of boys mentioned above. Stephen was still weak, and to give him a chance to get away Derek threw himself at the attackers, ended up so badly beaten that he tens of thousands of New Yorkers, including many of my friends, could not afford their meds.

I say he did all these things despite the energy it must have taken to maintain his assumed identity, although I wonder if it should be because. Because no matter how urgent the task, the kind of work that Derek and the other members of T&D and TAG did was, from any rational point of view, impossible. They were artists mostly, a few guppies, a few people like Derek too young to be anything yet. None of them had a medical background, and while they were trying to earn a living and trying to stay alive they were also giving themselves a crash course in virology and epidemiology and bureaucracy at the city, state, national, and international levels, and while they were educating themselves they were also taking on doctors, hospitals, pharmaceutical companies and insurance companies, the New York Stock Exchange and the National Institute of Allergies and Infectious Diseases and the Centers for Disease Control and the House of Representatives and the Senate and three successive presidents, and, with the help of a few thousand legmen, they won. They changed the way AIDS was talked about, the way it was studied and, most importantly, the way it was treated, and they did it all without giving in to despair or anomie, to the crazy-making frustration that any engagement with the health care bureaucracy is bound to engender, although in their case the frustration was magnified to an existential level and manifested itself as terror and rage. And they didn't give in to that terror either, or the rage. David Wojnarowicz's fantasy of shooting politicians with syringes filled with HIV-positive blood remained a fantasy, though whether that fantasy was a greater goad to politicians or AIDS activists is hard to say.

To suggest, however, that most of the members of T&D and TAG did what they did because they were HIV-positive is to forget that thousands upon thousands of HIV-positive people, many of whom were financially or educationally better suited for the task, did not fight in the same way, or at all. What I mean is, I don't believe it was empirically necessary for Derek to adopt the identity of an HIV-positive person in order to become the kind of AIDS activist he became. But he did, and he immersed himself in his role to such a degree that he put himself at risk of actually seroconverting. One of the great pleasures of our sex was that I didn't have to take my dick out of his mouth before I came, could let go of that last little piece of self-consciousness that safe sex requires and immerse myself, in all senses of the word, in sexual abandon, and not come back to the real world until the sound of Derek slurping up the last drops of my jizz reached my ears. I don't know if he also engaged in unprotected anal intercourse, but the fact that he was willing to let a stranger come in his mouth suggests the degree to which he had subsumed himself in his adopted identity. Suggests that there was a deeper process of self-abnegation and -invention involved, something that went beyond AIDS or sexuality to the inescapable contingency of the self—of, to use Leo Bersani's term, personhood, the existential status "that the law needs in order to discipline us, and ... to protect us." I won't say that Derek wanted to opt out of that discipline, or that protection, but his relationship to it was obviously conflicted, as if he had internalized the "crisis of representation" Simon Watney detailed in *Policing Desire* and amplified it into an identity—as if, to invert Andrew Sullivan's equation, he had come to believe that the only existence that had any meaning during a time of plague was as one of the infected. And though few people would have endorsed this position openly in the years before combination therapy became available, the number of gay men who hurriedly capitulated to HIV after 1996—their surrender guided (goaded?) by a new pornographic lexicon of "bug chasers" and "gift givers," the redefinition of "breeder" from a derogatory term for a heterosexual to an heroic name for a man who "gave" his HIV to his partner—suggests that from the beginning of the epidemic part of the fascination with AIDS was the desire to have it. To live with it? To die from it? I suspect it's probably neither, which is to say, I suspect the HIV these men wanted is the kind that Andrew Sullivan wrote about so winsomely rather than the actual virus in his body, the phantasmatic kind that brings "meaning" to life rather than sickness or pain or death—the kind that Derek had in other words, rather than the kind my friend Gordon had, and that killed him in 1996.

Which brings me back to my original question: did pretending to be HIV-positive help Derek do the work that he did, or was it incidental? I don't know the answer to that question, nor do I know how you'd ascertain it. Certainly not by asking Derek: why in the world would you believe something a pathological liar told you? What I do know is this: we were walking down 14th Street one day, either between First and A or A and B (I remember we passed the post office) and I was asking him why he'd stopped painting. There was more than a little uneasiness behind my question, because a part of me considered the time I spent as an activist as time I didn't spend writing, and vice versa. But I was surprised by Derek's answer. Art interfered with a direct experience of the world, Derek told me, and he wanted to experience the world firsthand. I asked him to elaborate and without missing a beat he pointed to a homeless man sleeping on the sidewalk. It was January, and the man was covered by newspapers, and Derek said, Art is like those newspapers. It covers up the real world, and the best that you can hope for is to see something through it. But whatever you see is going to be colored by art. Obscured by it. You're not going to see the real thing. You're going to see the artist's interpretation. Implicit in Derek's notion of art is the idea that it's always representational, of processes and ideas as much as objects and people. Most artists I know accept the idea that mimesis contains a greater or lesser degree of falsity even as its core—its intention— remains truthful, but what Derek seemed to be telling me was that, however much truth there is in representation, the *intention* is always false. To falsify. I didn't want to believe that then and, twenty-three years later, I still don't want to believe it. But I've always believed it—have believed it helplessly, which is why I've never even tried to make art that depicts the world as it actually is, but instead try to make art that points out its own biases, its own falseness, and the necessary illusions without which life is impossible. So that, if nothing else, the reader will know that what he's looking at is fiction, not history, and certainly not the world. I believed in 1991, when I was twenty-three years old, that those two or three dozen words were the single most important lesson anyone had ever taught me about the moral stakes of all forms of representation, political as well as aesthetic, and I believe it still. When I wrote in my journal that Derek was "a more authentic version of myself," I believed that he had genuinely endured the horrors, as a child of violence and a gay man in a viciously homophobic society, that I had only witnessed, and I believe it still. I believed that Derek lived his life by a moral code I only made feints at, and even after I found out that the biography he'd presented me was not just false, but malignantly so, in light of the pain his revelation inflicted on those men and women who had loved him, and fought beside him, and in some very real sense died for him, I continued to believe it.

I believe it still.

15

Everyone has his or her own library of that terrible time. For most people it probably consists of newspaper articles, a connect-the-dots narrative told in the epidemic's infamous acronyms: GRID and HTLV-III and PWA, KS and PCP and CMV, NIAID and ACT UP and WHO. Perhaps you saw *Angels in America* on Broadway or in a regional production; perhaps you saw or read *And the Band Played On* and maybe one or two more books: Paul Monette's *Becoming a Man*, Michael Cunningham's *A Home at the End of the World*. A small group of us devoured everything we came across, from the crackpot theories of Peter Duesberg to the radical epidemiology of Michael Callen, along with the hundreds of novels, memoirs, and polemics that charted the emotional, intellectual, moral, and symbolic space between these poles. To another, equally select group, AIDS literature was a catalog of titles perused on the shelves of other people's apartments, perhaps during a cocktail party, perhaps during a hookup when the host was in the bathroom. Two or three books were regarded as a sign of admirable interest in current events, a certain depth of character even; but too many could provoke nervous speculation: *Is he ... ?* and, even more alarmingly: *Should I ... ?*

To claim that some of these ways of reading about AIDS are better than others is to miss the point of writing about AIDS. Literature facilitates empathy as well as understanding, and for that reason the mere fact of a book's existence can effect extraordinary personal change. But because literature can only enfold the present within its scope by displacing it in time, it has the effect of rendering the events it describes contained, finished, *past*. As a consequence, fiction and drama, memoir and poetry and history serve first and foremost as memorials: to worlds lost or worlds that never were. For the literature of a disease whose final chapter was for fifteen years almost certain death, there was a resonant if morbid appropriateness to this translation. Many of those early texts are what might be called hopeful elegies: books in which protagonists declined and often died but a community soldiered on, and even grew stronger in the face of so much desolation. Whether you think literature facilitated the political transformation of gay life or merely benefited from it depends on how cynical you are; certainly it didn't have the same effect for IV-drug users, nor again for Haitians or African-Americans, let alone Africans. In either case, the first decade and a half of the AIDS epidemic produced a concentrated body of books, plays, poems, and essays, many of which now seem, like the devastating interval they chronicle, a part of ancient history.

My own library of AIDS literature begins with the phrase "Mark was ill, dying perhaps; say no more" in the excerpt from Robert Ferro's *Second Son* that appears in the first *Men on Men* anthology, published in 1986.[*] That sentence, hinged on the almost perversely optimistic use of the word "perhaps," swings between the incontrovertible facts of

---

[*]Ferro cut the "say no more" by the time *Second Son* was published in 1988, an excision I've wondered about off and on for the past twenty-eight years, sometimes regarding it as a kind of victory, sometimes a capitulation. I wanted to ask him why he removed it, but by the time *Second Son* came out Ferro was also dead.

illness and death on the one hand, and, on the other, the idea that literature might succeed in capturing the overwhelming nature of "the plague" only by avoiding it, or at least not tackling it head on. Hence the decision not to name the disease in this and many other stories and novels of the mid-eighties, as well as the fact that death, though never denied, was left out of the text far more often than it was in life. But beginnings imply endings, and for me the inevitable conclusion came with Rebecca Brown's *The Gifts of the Body* in 1994. The diffuse storylines of Brown's narrative reflected the changing demographics of the epidemic, and Brown was also one of the last writers who managed to avoid what had by then become the nearly universal practice of ennobling sick people merely because of affliction. Allen Barnett's "HIVs" and "HIV-nots" proved the first in a long series of puns, as organizations took names like ACT UP, Body Positive, and Visual AIDS and writers titled their books *Eighty-Sixed*, *A Matter of Life and Sex*, *Love Undetectable*, and *Cocktails*. God knows I wasn't immune to this trend: the original title of this section of this essay was "Preaching to the Converted." It served as the foreword to an anthology of AIDS fiction called *Vital Signs*, which was part of Transmissions, a series of reprinted books about AIDS. I'm only grateful that I came up with the title *Shoot to Kill* after my first novel had gone to press.

But the main reason *The Gifts of the Body* comes at the end of my personal list of books about AIDS is because it was published just before protease inhibitors and combination therapy radically changed the course of the illness. These treatments didn't obliterate mortality but they did, for those who could get them, attenuate it, rendering the already nebulous "meaning" of dying and disease that much harder to express. Eighteen years later, literature has yet to find a way to communicate that ambiguity, perhaps because contemporary writers have shirked their responsibility, perhaps because it's still too soon, or perhaps simply because it can't. This isn't to say that good and even great books about AIDS stopped being produced after 1995 and '96, but they appeared in isolation rather than in concert, fueled by individual rather than collective consciousnesses. The moral, mortal urgency that set fire to the pens of a half generation of writers tempered as death eased its hold on our lives as well as our imaginations, and though this is in many ways a victory, it has the taste of defeat. For too many, AIDS has become just one more of life's hardships borne by other people— people who live in other cities or other countries; who lead other ways of life; who are other people's concern, other people's problem. But to spend too much time wishing that contemporary books about AIDS were as "good" as the ones that came out before 1996, as potent, as numerous, as widely read, is to miss what should be an obvious point: AIDS didn't happen to make literature better. Literature just happened to get better in response to AIDS, at least for a while. Though that body of work may not tell us exactly where we are now, it does tell us how we got here—how

with gluts of sex, death, and debauchery. And so, just as World War I gave us the Lost Generation, AIDS gave us Generation X, and its literary expression, New Narrative. It was this movement that inspired both Heather and myself at the beginning of our careers.

Terms like "Gen X" and "New Narrative" imply a self-awareness that smacks of backward glances. At the time there was just the fragmented reality of political demonstrations and academic conferences, independent bookstores selling books published by small presses and guerilla xeroxing for those who couldn't afford even those cheap paperbacks, handmade zines instead of the piss elegance of *McSweeney's*. In those heady days before hipsters purchased poverty like a fashion statement, the magazine of choice for young writers like Heather and me was *Between C & D*, an accordion fold of dot-matrix printer paper that came in a plastic bag, and toward the end there was also a press, High Risk, whose oversaturated Rex Ray collages were the antidote to the bright kitschy covers Knopf's Vintage line was making all the rage. "New Narrative" was a term that floated around this milieu and, like the term "PWA," only had meaning if you were already acquainted with it, and even today the genre remains hard to quantify. Less postmodern than post-punk, it had no time for the inebriating irony that had paralyzed American literature in the 1970s. Fear, doubt, and uncertainty were plowed through, not confidently, but of necessity. History had regained its solidity in the most banal, terrifying manner—by asserting its right to kill you—and in response literature returned to the Homeric mode of bearing witness. Sentences were pared down, plots streamlined, self-examination and self-expression voiced in a present tense that measured the past in punches and orgasms, metered the future in breaths rather than years. There was no choate vision of survival, nor even a belief that survival was possible, and as a result New Narrative didn't have a universal form as much as a unifying ethos, one in which desperation tinged success every bit as much as it did failure.

Both Heather and I came late to this movement, publishing our first novels in 1994 and 1993, respectively, but we were too young to realize that the writers we admired weren't our peers but our progenitors. Our teachers. In those days literary "generations" flashed by as rapidly as shuffling cards, and largely as a result of the efforts of writers who are only now reaching their fifties and sixties (if they're still alive) we were able to launch our careers not with small presses but with Farrar Straus and Giroux in my case, and Doubleday's boutique Nan Talese imprint in Heather's. But though we didn't realize it at the time, Heather and I were betweeners, aesthetically aligned with a group of writers who existed out of the mainstream even as we ourselves were proof that the mainstream could . . . what? Open its arms and expand its definition of normal? Suspend moral judgment where money could be made? We suspected the latter but operated as though the former were the case, but in the end motive matters less than results. It was only after the fact that we understood our election was predicated on the demise of the writing upon which we'd been weaned, the marginalization of it, by which I mean that critics neglected the literary merits of *House Rules* and its predecessors in favor of a new obsession: "victim art," as the reactionary critic Katie Roiphe called it, an epithet that became the hatchet with which all art that portrayed personal suffering without a concomitant "hopeful" moral was cut down—especially art that dealt with sexual abuse and AIDS. The furore reached its nadir in December 1994, when the *New Yorker*'s dance critic, Arlene Croce, refused to see *Still/Here* by choreographer Bill T. Jones on the grounds that such "victim art" was "unreviewable."

WELL. WHAT AMERICA can't exclude it absorbs, dilutes, mutes. The quasi-religious fantasy that a pattern hiding behind the chaos will emerge occasionally into view (i.e., the Joycean epiphany) reared its head yet again, and denied New Narrative's single existential truth: that the end of life implies nothing more tangible than an earlier beginning, and art can do little besides measure the distance from the loss. In the end, New Narrative's effect was different from what one might have expected, as a varied cohort of writers incorporated aspects of its sensibility into a neutered postmodernism. Much of the New Narrative writing it superseded has been denigrated to second-class status now, while most AIDS writing teeters on the verge of being forgotten or lost. When, in 2011, I created a Wikipedia page listing about 250 books with significant AIDS content, the page was soon deleted, with the justifying arguments ranging from "Are any of these books bestsellers?" to "I do not see any encycolpedic [sic] value for such a list" and "The Category:HIV/AIDS in literature [which at the time listed all of thirty-two books] suffices for works that are of note."

What does survive shows up here and there like pieces of samizdat from another era, another world even, another life. I've always loved samizdat. The romance of the phenomenon, yes, but also the word itself, largely because the first time I remember hearing it was at ACT UP. The term was applied to the vast stacks of photocopies that we picked up on our way into the Monday night meeting: treatment guidelines, drug studies, bureaucratic analyses, meeting schedules, action plans, contact lists, party flyers, and announcements of events ranging from performances and gallery openings to house parties and memorial services. This collection was never referred to as anything other than "the table" (even though it usually spread over two or three), a twelve- or eighteen-foot-long print banquet down both sides of which several hundred gay men and lesbians, nearly indistinguishable in their Doc Martens and Levi's and sloganned T-shirts, bent their spiky or shaved heads and served themselves and one another with the ordered geniality of an Amish wedding. I was a pretentious but undereducated twenty-two-year-old who didn't want to admit he was unfamiliar with a term that had the clannish (ap)peal of jargon, the ignorance of which marked him out as neophyte or, worse, interloper. What I mean is, I heard the word in my head as "same-as-that," or "sameasthat" really, which led me to think of it as an assertion of status: though these stapled stacks of paper, most written by people with no political background or scientific or journalistic training, lacked the credentials and durability of bound books, they were nevertheless the lifeblood of AIDS activism. Sameasthat: most of the table's contents survived for only a few hours or a few days, ended up buried in boxes in closets, attics, garages, but to me they were the real library of AIDS, and the glossily jacketed books that trickled out of FSG and Nan Talese were the table's supplements rather than the other way around.

The single most significant piece of sameasthat in my life, however, and by far the most resonant document of my AIDS library, came into my world about nine months before I joined ACT UP. It was 1989 and I was in my last semester of college. I worked in a used bookstore, ostensibly to save up for my impending move to the city, though in fact most of my salary went right back into my boss's till, since I must have bought three or five or a dozen books every week I worked there. At some point that spring Frank, my boss, brought in a cache of hundreds of opera records. The jackets were faded and tattered and spotted with mold, the discs filthy but, beneath their layer of dust, nearly pristine.

Their condition attested to a long period of heavy but respectful use and a second interval of less than benign neglect. Each disc had to be taken from its sleeve and washed by hand, a delicate but monotonous job for a twenty-one-year-old who had zero interest in opera, and I was relieved as much as intrigued when five wrinkled sheets of onionskin fell out of a gaudy sixties or seventies-era case containing Bizet's *Carmen*. The sheets were as well-worn as the cardboard that had held them, unruled and covered with florid and, as I thought, old ladyish handwriting, still bright blue despite the fact that the date at the top of the first page read 26 September 1965—the day written before the month, in the European manner. "My dear Gino" was the only other thing I was able to make out before I put the letter aside and returned to the task at hand, and I didn't decipher the rest until later that evening, alone in my dorm room, my heart quickening as each successive sentence revealed a love story that seemed as stark and gaudy as an opera, as melodramatic and doomed and unreal. Except this love, between a man named Gino and another named Jean-gabriel, *was* real, or at any rate it had been, twenty-four years earlier, and the next day I asked Frank—as nonchalantly as possible, and without mentioning the letter—if he remembered the name of the person whose records he'd purchased the day before.

It was a time in my life when omens seemed to appear everywhere, conflicting, confusing, beguiling. "You have terrible taste in literature," my boss told me after perusing the stacks of books I'd set aside (almost all of which had been published within the last five years), and he gave me a copy of Frank Conroy's *Stop-Time*. My boss knew I wanted to be a writer, but there was no way he could have been aware I'd applied to the Iowa Writers' Workshop, still less that I'd receive my rejection letter, signed by Conroy, on the very day I finished his memoir (which I loved, and which made the rejection feel personal and portentous). Then there was the matter of sex. I'd waited a long time before coming out, and on the very day I finally allowed myself to have sex my watch stopped. This was the only watch I'd ever owned, the watch I'd bought when I'd come to college two and a half years earlier, the watch that signified my desire to be on time for my adult life, and its battery gave out *while I was getting fucked without a condom*, and practically at the witching hour to boot: 11:57 P.M. And now there was this letter, which I wanted to see as a totem not just validating my sexuality but repudiating the augury of my watch's stopped hands. Which is to say: my first sexual experience a year earlier remained my only one, and my conception of "the gay life" was mediated entirely through literature. I was the same age as the letter's recipient and, like him, lived in New Jersey, but my sights were trained on the "N.Y. temptations" to which I would be immigrating in little over a month. What I mean is, I didn't know if I wanted to meet Gino or to be Gino, only that I didn't want my fate decided by a $30 Swatch.

He died of AIDS! Frank told me brightly, then blushed and dropped his eyes. He'd seen the obituary in the *Times*, he remembered, and somehow this didn't surprise me: the fact that Gino was dead, I mean, not that he'd merited a *Times* obituary. The condition of his records, for one thing, and the fact that they were opera, which I associated with death (not with funerals per se, but with death scenes in movies, the kind of murder and mourning and revenge that insists on a soundtrack). And then, well, forty-four-year-old gay men were dying in legions in 1989. It was something Italian, Frank continued. Gianni, no, Gino, that was it! Gino . . . Gino . . . ? But he couldn't remember the last name. He looked for the paper but it was gone. He racked his brain but the only other things he remembered were that Gino had appeared in a Warhol movie, and that later he'd had something to do with music, though Frank didn't remember in what capacity. As it turned out these were clues enough, though I didn't realize it for another five years—five years during which I moved to the city and joined ACT UP to end the AIDS crisis and left ACT UP to start my writing career. The signs continued to appear, the most significant of which occurred when the magazine I was working for went out of business and I ran into Derek Link, who offered me the ticket to San Francisco that he'd bought for his boyfriend (the boyfriend he'd dumped me for), who'd just dumped him. It was a trip I couldn't have taken if I'd had a job, and while I was away my agent got an offer from FSG for my first novel. My new editor's assistant turned out to be a

Warhol fan, which prompted me to mention the letter I'd found—to mention the date and the name Gino and his appearance in Warhol's films—and without pausing Jennifer said, "Gino Piserchio." Are you sure? I asked. I think he did some music too. This only strengthened Jennifer's conviction: Gino Piserchio was the boy on the bed with Edie Sedgwick in Warhol's *Beauty No. 2*, she told me, and, later, the composer of the music for *Ciao! Manhattan*, which, like *Carmen*, and like Bizet's own life, and Piserchio's, was yet another story of early death—in this case Sedgwick's, whose obituary appears at the end of the film. As a final confirmation we looked up the date of Piserchio's death: March 22, 1989.

Of Jean-gabriel's identity I remain ignorant, although I have to confess I've never searched for it very hard. His letter is beautiful and forlorn and beseeching and even a little creepy, but it is also a failure, at least in its intended sense. I'm forty-six now, two years older than Gino when he died, I've outgrown my youthful resistance to opera; and Gino was a musician, and an educated one at that: he went to Mannes College of Music and did graduate work at Columbia; he's considered one of the first musicians to fully exploit the Moog synthesizer. He was, in other words, a music connoisseur, and a connoisseur wouldn't keep Jean-gabriel's letter in a copy of *Carmen* if its suit had been successful. Carmen is the girl who says, *When will I love you? I don't know. Maybe never, maybe tomorrow.* She's a liberated girl, or at any rate a lawless one: she works in a factory, she smokes, she slashes the face of Manuelita to end a fight that she—Carmen—started, then flirts with her guard until he lets her out of jail. When Don José is imprisoned for freeing Carmen she takes pity on him, even thinks she's falling in love. She asks him to turn his back on his duty and join her as a gypsy, a vagabond, an outlaw. Circumstances keep them together for a while but Carmen quickly grows bored: Don José is, clearly, a good citizen, and Carmen is a free spirit—or, as she puts it in the opera's most famous aria: *Love is a gypsy's child. It has never known the law.* Soon enough Carmen throws Don José over for the bullfighter Escamillo and, in the grip of a madness that can only be whipped up by spurned love and a full orchestra, Don José stabs Carmen rather than relinquish her to another man. *It is I who has killed her*, he confesses to the crowd, *Ah Carmen, my adored Carmen!* The opera's last lines have eerie—icky—resonance with something Chuck Wien says at one point in *Beauty No. 2*. Edie jostles Gino and he chokes on his drink. "Nice Gino," Chuck admonishes Edie. "Don't let Gino die. Sweet Gino. We're not going to let him die." "He won't!" Edie protests, a little petulant, a little forlorn, her upper-class consonants crisp despite the amount of alcohol she's consumed. "He won't?" Chuck prompts, and Edie shakes her head. She looks at Gino. "You won't want to die," she says, consonants crisp, vowels round and full as embroidered bolsters even as the words formed from these cultured phonemes don't quite make sense, and in response Gino lays a hand on her naked calf in a gesture that could mean anything, or nothing at all.

Jean-gabriel says in his first paragraph that he's responding to a letter Gino wrote him after two years of silence, and one can't help but wonder what made Gino reach out after all that time to a man he met only once. It's 1965, remember: *Beauty No. 2* has just come out, and Edie Sedgwick has been declared Girl of the Year. Twenty-one-year-old Gino must have basked in the glow she and Andy and the other Superstars gave off, must have felt like one himself. (Edie: "And then you said he wasn't Beauty No. 1." Chuck: "Nobody said he wasn't Beauty No. 1. But that's true, now that you say it.") But he *is* beautiful. Everyone, men and women, want him, and more than a few get him, but through them all he remembers the French boy he fled from two years before and, in a fit of guilt or hubris or, who knows, genuine romance, decides to write him. Who knows what happened by the time Jean-gabriel's answer came back? Another man maybe (Chuck: "The new is better. That's what we live for. The new.") or maybe a woman—Piserchio and heiress Gillian Spreckels Fuller married in 1972, then divorced three years later. At any rate whatever impulse had prompted Gino to write didn't survive long enough for him to succumb to Jean-gabriel's heart-on-his-sleeve, cards-on-the-table reply. But the urgency of the Frenchman's words triggered something in its recipient, nostalgia maybe, a curiosity about what might have been, a desire to be worthy of the kind of love it offered, and eventually the letter took up residence in the sleeve of *Carmen*. I imagine Gino pulling it out every

Love stays away; you wait and wait;
when least expected, there it is!
All around you, swift, swift,
it comes, goes, then it returns.
You think you hold it fast, it flees;
you think you're free, it holds you fast.
Oh, love! Love! Love! Love!

Sunday 26 September 1965

My dear Gino,

What a wonderful surprise! You cannot imagine how much you made me happy receiving your very long letter. Not too long, of course. I was feeling 2 years younger and happy. Thanks, thank you very much. Go on. I am always astonished with your letters: I cannot understand how a so young boy like you is able to write down so lovely and intelligent letters.

And the wonderful snapshots! I appreciate very much that you took care to go to the post office and to put into an envelope so nice pictures. I looked at them a lot of times and I have to tell you which were my thoughts:

The first one is that I want to see you again as soon as possible. I was hesitating to fly to this N.Y. this summer but I had no real purpose without seeing you. Nothing could enjoy me more than to take you in my arms. I would like only to be sure that it's the same for you as it could be. I am a little bit afraid to be so excited to meet you again when I think of the short period during which we were together. I remember quite well that I cried a lot when you left me at the station on my last week-end in the Big City. Do you? And I had difficulty to forgive you to have left me alone but you explained to me the reasons.

The second one is that you look nearly the same. I say nearly, because you look taller and thinner. The surprising difference is your long hair! To any one you are still very good-looking and the most important thing is that I find the same nice boy when I have the great pleasure to see you again. I love your pictures and if you have other ones don't hesitate to send me them. I'll keep them very carefully. I am laughing a little bit about your long hair. Don't consider that as a criticism but I prefer you with shorter hair. You have probably to do it for your magazine snapshots. Last week I said to one of my young accountants: "Do you want really to be one of the Beatles." He blushed and promised to go to the hair-dresser, but he did not. May I confess that I have longer hair but still shorter than the young beautifuls in Paris?

The third thought provoked by your beautiful face is that I am pleased you are a little bit older. As you have written it you have thought of the problems of life, of love, of your way of living, of the purpose you have to follow. When I met you I was convinced after a few days that you could not arrest your attention on one person: Jean-gabriel, but that it was necessary for you, at your age, to know other boys, the gay life and all the aspects of the way of living in the world and it was painful for me. You did and I cannot criticize you. I regretted it but I had not the right to do it. You had to compare between them a lot of things, a lot of persons and only after you could stabilize yourself. This moment can happen when you are 20, 30, or 40, even more. It depends on persons. Have you now enough elements of comparison and do you know now partly what want? I hope so and I hope you have the desire to live a quieter life, a more interesting life, more attractive and that I could have a place in this life. You have to tell me frankly which one. What is the use to meet a lot of boys, to scatter his love, to kill his capacity of love finally? You have to choice your way: you have a lot of abilities: don't spoil your life! Build something nice and great. And for that love is necessary, real love and not a lot of affairs. But with whom would you like to try? You're more confident now because what you wrote about love and your "neurotic needs" is very well deliberated and true. Believe me, a French boy, at your age, could not analyze a problem in such an intelligent way. And I like intelligent persons. You say that you don't live only for the "immediate satisfaction of your neurotic needs," that it has taken for you two years difficulties: no job, no flat. But could we accept that somebody has sex for interest?

Are you in New Jersey for a long time? It's much better to be away from N.Y. temptations.

I understand that you could come to Europe. Tell me as soon as possible which are your plans. Is it necessary to write that you are invited at my place? I'll get a new car next month, a convertable one, and we could do together some nice trip through Europe.

I have more to say about your music, about your job as a model. It will be for the next letter.

My dear Gino, I seldom wrote a long letter with such a pleasure. Be good. Write soon.

Love and love from your Jean-gabriel

16

I have to tell you
You have to tell me
Love is necessary
Is it necessary to write
I have more to say
There is no question of language

And yet, in the end, that's all there is. Questions. Language. More to say. Because language is like a sense: it's like seeing, hearing, smelling, touching, though perhaps it's most like tasting. It's a way of capturing something and bringing it inside yourself. But this capture is only a beginning. Words, like food, have to be digested, and definitions are like flavors. What you taste when you eat lasagna and what I taste when I eat lasagna and what you mean by love and what I mean by love have both similarities and differences—they may even have more similarities than they have differences, but it's the differences that divide us, and it's these divisions that stories like this one hope to narrow. And so, to close, one more story:

My first boyfriend, Jean-Claude Robert Breach, was a beautiful man with eyes the color of a clear brown-bottomed pool of water and, when I knew him, a fresh pink scar that brought out the line of his left cheekbone. The time of our love affair encompassed a lazy summer in which neither of us had jobs or classes or anything to do besides participate in ACT UP and Queer Nation demonstrations and be with each other. I remember one of those summer evenings after a long hot afternoon together: we ended up in the Bar on Second Avenue and 4th Street—the same bar where I met Derek Link and where I broke up with Patrick Smith (RIP), the same bar that today is a fake British pub—and because money was short we bought only one bottle of water to share between us. The bottle was in Jean-Claude's hand and he took the first drink. I expected him to hand it to me but instead he pulled me close with his free hand and pressed his lips to mine and passed me the water that was in his mouth. I knew immediately that

I shouldn't swallow but pass it back to him, and I did, and he passed it back to me, and the water moved back and forth between us, its temperature warming, its taste changing as it mixed with his saliva and my saliva, its volume shrinking with each pass as some of it trickled down our throats and some dribbled down our chins, and when at last the first mouthful was gone he took another drink and the process began again. I remember this as the most *shared* experience of my entire life. I believed I was tasting the water exactly as Jean-Claude tasted it and that he was tasting it exactly as I did and, though I usually think that every cell in my body that might have been affected by that water has long since been sloughed off, I remind myself that the brain is made of cells, and I let myself believe that those few sips of water did indeed change me forever. Not just mentally, I mean, but physically. In an era when the term "bodily fluids" carried a whiff of the cemetery and virtually every physical interaction between gay men was mediated by a discussion of its relative risk, the water that Jean-Claude offered me was analogue and antidote to the semen that, two years earlier, my first sexual partner had shot in my ass with no regard for my safety, or his own.

I'm not sure if this story is phrased as an answer or just another question. I do know I would like to eroticize our knowledge of the world and each other. And so, rather than conclude by writing "these words have left my mouth and entered your ear" (because they haven't, after all, they've left my hand and entered your eye) I write instead: the water has left my mouth and entered yours. Now you have

2

THIRTEEN ECSTASIES
OF THE SOUL

for Gordon Armstrong
1960–1996

Declaration:

ON LEAVING HOME

Tell your mother that you love her but make her no oath of loyalty. Let her clasp your hands between hers for only a moment and then pull free. Shake your father's hand firmly then, then shake your brother's, then bend down low to kiss your sister on the cheek. Hug your mother, and your sister, and your brother when he finally comes forward, and nod to your father, who stands with his hands behind his back. You know they expect words from you but don't give them away. Tell them goodbye. Tell them you look forward to seeing them again but don't say when. Tell them that today there are only starting points. The journey on which you embark has neither direction nor destination; the search that you will make has neither method nor object. If they persist in questioning you step away from them. Scratch your head, and smile, and tell them that you are a man now.

1. Sloth

In the morning, when you awaken, the light that fills your room is that of a sun pushing through a sky thick with clouds. You hear the light sound of drizzle outside, and on the exposed skin of your shoulders and neck and head you feel damp cold air, and you pull the light blanket a little higher. For a moment, you tell yourself, for just a moment you'll stay in bed. In a moment you reset the alarm for an hour hence, and when that hour comes you push it back another hour. You half sleep during those two hours: your body is rested, what it's doing now is languishing; you merely lie in bed. Your eyes are closed, your mind neither dreaming nor focusing on anything as definite as a thought. When the alarm rings again you shut it off. By now you've abandoned the day, and you turn the clock around, turn off the ringer on the bedside phone, turn your body over and feel, more than anything else, the pressure of your pierced right nipple on the mattress. But masturbation, you feel, would be wrong, a break in the pact you're making with laziness, and, slowly, you convince your body to relax. You're hungry, but when you realize you're not going to do any-thing that requires energy that hunger becomes less important, ignorable, eventually unnoticeable; in the same way the pressure from your bladder recedes. The rainy day passes: sometimes you lie awake and sometimes you sleep; when you sleep you dream sometimes, and your dreams are deep and vivid but disappear each time you wake. When you're awake you notice the gradations of light in the room, morning's gray, afternoon's silver, evening's almost brown shadows, and then, inevitably, it's black again. There's no strength anywhere in your body; the urge to stay in bed all day, whatever else it was, wasn't vampiric: you're tired, and ready to sleep the night away. You set the alarm for tomorrow, and in the few minutes before you fall into a sound sleep you have the only clear thought you've had all day (because your mind, too, your mind was lazy today). You have done nothing today, absolutely nothing. But you haven't wasted this day; you have, instead, erased it. When tomorrow comes you will be no closer to death than you were yesterday.

2. Hunger

That morning I put on last night's clothes out of deference to you, who had no choice, and so, reeking of cigarette smoke and smelling also of sweat and beer and poppers, we entered a hot bright morning in search of food. You wore jeans, I remember, and an old tight T-shirt that had once been blue; your hair was more red than I'd realized, and the sunlight brought out the freckles in your skin. What was on your feet? At the restaurant we ordered coffee and water and orange juice. We ordered eggs and potatoes, and while we waited we ate the loaf of bread they'd left us, layering each slice with a thick film of butter. When our breakfast came we ordered more coffee and more juice; the waiter filled our water glasses, brought us more bread. We mashed the scrambled eggs and hash browns together and forked them in yellow lumps onto pieces of buttered bread. We laughed as we ate, I remember, but we didn't talk, and bits of food sprayed across the table; when our forks scraped across our empty plates we looked at each other and then ordered more: more eggs, more potatoes—omelettes, this time, and French fries—more coffee, more juice, more bread, too, and a couple of those corn muffins we saw advertised on a blackboard. The waiter attempted a joke, but something about the way we wielded our forks and knives stopped him. Perhaps he was just driven away by the farts leaking from both of us: by then, peristalsis had produced in me a tremendous urge to shit, and I knew it must have been much worse for you. The waiter brought the coffee and juice first, then the bread. We discovered a jar of strawberry jam and ate a spoonful with each bite of bread. We dunked our muffins in our coffee and when they broke apart we fished out the yellow-brown dumplings with our spoons. We blackened our omelettes with pepper and drank drafts of water to cool our throats, we swirled fries into a spiral of mustard and ketchup, and as I finished my coffee I discovered an inch of slushy sugar at the bottom of the cup that I let dribble down my throat. The waiter approached warily. Will there be anything else, boys? We looked at each other and smiled. There were bread crumbs in your goatee, green herbs stuck in your teeth. I watched you press your finger into a piece of food that had spewed from one of our mouths, then bring your finger to your tongue. We hadn't spoken all morning except to order, and you left it up to me now. We'd gone far past the point of satiety, but each bite, each swallow, each burning burp had carried a hint of revelation, and all I could say was "More."

3. Shit

Who was the culprit? The man you sucked off in the bar's bathroom last Saturday, or the trick you met on the street in the middle of the week, the one who'd decorated his apartment in Catholic kitsch and kneeled in front of you like an altar boy? Perhaps it was the man who fucked you without a rubber beside the indoor swimming pool in his apartment building, the smell of chlorine in your nostrils, the cold tiles irritating your back, the guilt you felt almost but not quite overriding the pleasure of his unfettered cock moving inside you. It doesn't really matter: you're trapped now, on your toilet, your stomach swelling with gases like pseudocyesis and watery shit leaking from your ass, wishing you had followed your mother's advice and become a priest and waiting for the erythromycin to take effect. When the diarrhea is on hold your body relaxes and your mind wanders; you imagine amoebae moving inside of you by means of pseudopodia, as your encyclopedia told you, false feet, a protrusion of cytoplasm that is both a means of locomotion and of consumption. It feels like they're stampeding; what's left for them to eat? When the diarrhea starts again your intestines cramp visibly; there's Compazine for that but it's not working yet. You close your eyes against the burning pain in your guts and your ass; it's a cliché, but it feels like lava is moving through your body. After the umpteenth episode, when you have wiped yourself clean with wet toilet paper to soothe the rash on your buttocks and flushed the toilet, you open your eyes and realize as you look at the unfamiliar walls of your bathroom that when your eyes had been shut your mind had been shut as well. Not just shut, but shut off. You remember it as a blank moment of time; you remember now a succession of these blank moments, reaching back into the early hours of the morning when the diarrhea first struck. They are like bricks, these blank spots, and together they form a wall through which you can't see, over which you can't climb, around which you can't walk or run. You feel trapped then, by that wall, by the undeniable feeling of wellness moving into your body, by the inadequacy of the grammar you possess to describe the wall and the wellness. You know that while you were building that wall you were able to see beyond it, but now you can't remember what you saw, and as you wait in vain for the next bout of diarrhea you realize that the body doesn't always succumb to illness: sometimes it yearns for it. It embraces it with a protrusion of false limbs and pulls it inside itself, and in so doing takes you, if only for a little while, beyond the confines of this world, and into another.

4. Love

Spring

The days pass one by one. On top of the mountain the sky is always clear and the wind always humid. Each evening at sunset, when the heat breaks, he becomes your sun. He pulls you into orbit around him; the heat is from his body, the light from his eyes. You try to take all of him but he's too much for one man to handle. His surplus flows from you in fluids, in breath, in words, and it's inevitable that in their rovings his hands, his eyes, his mouth shall retrieve the parts of him that you slough off. This is the cycle: day into night into day, him into you into him. But the light and the darkness remain discrete and distinct, while you and he blend together, become inseparable, indistinguishable, like lichen. It's pointless to say that if you remove one the other will die: there is no one, there is no other. This is not the general product of love; this is the product of your love, of your ecstasy. Some people give birth to babies. You give birth to each other.

Summer

Germination was a tender touching process, soon over: seeds split like broken zippers, shoots push into darkness, trusting that this way lies the sun. Growth seems a funny purposeless thing until suddenly the closed petals of lust burst open, revealing the naked desire of need and want, of love. In your thirst you drink the poisoned blood of the one you have named lover. In your hunger you lick the shit from his ass and the pus from his sores and the fungus that grows in his eyes and mouth and feet and fingers. His drool is your faucet, his piss your shower, his cum marks the end of your days. You take the pain of his every illness and injury inside you; a thousand times you take the seed of death from him and let it bloom within your body. In the end the strength of the need of your love exhausts him, chokes him as the vine chokes the tree. He withers within your grasp, and together you crumple to the ground.

Fall

He will call you when the crows fly thick through the night. You will go out and walk under cover of darkness and falling feathers and caw-caw-cawing for carrion. There will be neither light to see nor air to breathe nor room in the thick atmosphere to push out words, and the only thing you can trust is his hand in yours. Its bones are thin, frail, light, the bones of a bird, and they pull you on and on, past your town, past the farms that surround your town, into the empty uncultivated fields that lie beyond the farms. In long cold dry grass he will lay you down, and his hands fluttering across the expanse of your skin are a bellows, blowing away your clothes, igniting the coals that, for him, are always smoldering in your body. He has given birth to you once again, and now you reach for him and attempt to mirror his passion: he kisses you and you open your mouth, he ties your arms to the ground with grass and you don't pull against the weak roots, he lifts your legs and aims his cock at your asshole. The muscles in your ass shiver and try to pull him inside of you but before he lets you have him he plays a language game. "An exaltation of larks," he spits into your ear, "an ostentation of peacocks, a pride of lions." He lifts his head then, and you see that he is looking at the dark shapes flying overhead. "A murder of crows!" you scream, and he fucks you then, and morning never comes. And if that's not love it will have to do, until the real thing comes along.

Winter

You lost him one night in a tangle of sheets. He disappeared into a drift of snow and was consumed by a pile of paper. When the white had finally finished its task you found yourself with only frozen toes and a damp hollow in your bed. Yesterday's news is your only information. Cheap sentiments fill your mind, false memories in which your life together is reduced to a discount vacation package of pastoral picnics, Caribbean cruises, and sweet lustless sex. Outside your window the world is frozen solid; the only movements are signs of further decay. Tree limbs snap in the wind, squirrels eat their frostbitten toes in a vain effort to stay alive. This stillness is your only consolation, for you tell yourself that as long as the world remains motionless you will move no farther from him than you already are. Cold comfort, this, for when he left you his leaving was absolute. Eventually you leave your bed, your bedroom, your home: you cover the white skin that covers your body with clothing and walk into the fields west of your house. They are bare now, covered with frosty soil so hard that it chips under your feet like shale. But these fields aren't fallow. Last fall you watched the farmer plant his wheat, and during the warm afternoons you could almost see it grow. When the frost came it died, but you know that all it awaits is the spring thaw, when it will burst from the ground. In the middle of all this you stand. You watch the slow minuet of objects and shadows. Your own shadow curls around your body like a vine as the moon moves through the sky. I watch you from the other side of the window. If you ever come back I will tell you what I can see from here, which perhaps you cannot. For your lover, Gordon, *you* are the frozen earth. The façade of death is only temporary, and I promise you that one day you will both be born again.

to be; there is just a set of obvious correspondences to memorize, to offer up or respond to. Yellow means piss, brown shit, black and blue, well, they mean black and blue, and more individual concerns—how dominant is dominant, how submissive submissive—are communicated through the strength of a stare or the coyness of an averted glance, through bearing, through signals that, even if you spoke the language here, you would still pick up on. When do you notice the dark narrow descending stairway at the back of the bar? You're not sure. It's been in your peripheral vision for some time now, registered like a cataract by your eye but not your mind. Once you see it your eyes keep return- ing to it. Men go down; they don't seem to come back up; but you don't go down. You make yourself wait, drink another beer, and then another. You let yourself imagine, just a little, what might be going on below you, and you move closer so that you smell more clearly the sex smell, hear occasionally a slap or a groan. Finally you go down, one steep step at a time. Immediately it's darker: walls and pipes and other things register only as motionless shadows, men as moving ones. They are stripped now of even the simple code you were able to observe upstairs. The first thing you realize is that this doesn't bother you, and the second thing you realize is that it's actually a continuation of what was happening above: here, in this bar, you and these men are losing individuality, becoming more and more alike, images that reflect each other in one sense and, in another, partially discrete pieces, like tentacles, of some larger whole that is represented most clearly by the bar but that is not, you feel, confined to the bar itself; and the third thing you realize is that someone is running his hand along the crack of your ass. For an instant you surrender and push into the hand, listening to the sounds of other men, watching their coupling shadows, but then you pull away and move deeper into the basement. You walk through the network of small rooms and narrow hallways, thinking as you go that with a little paint, better lighting, several well-placed area rugs—on second thought, better make that wall-to-wall—this could be a nice place to live. When you have made your way through all the rooms and all the men you find a place to stand, and stand there. The men who had been close to you move closer. You look into blank faces at expressions you can't make out and offer a smile to the man nearest you—a tall man, broad shouldered, with long white arms and big hands encased in black gloves—but then you realize he probably can't see your smile, so you offer him your body instead. You press up against him and feel the hair on his chest and his soft flat stomach, and probe at the hidden message of his leather-coated crotch. You're prepared to back away if he indicates that he doesn't want you but he stands firm, and when you have fitted your body as tightly to his as you can he places one hand on your ass and the other on your head. He tips your head back and kisses you, surprising you with a short moustache and a long smoky tongue, and then he works his fingers as deeply into your ass as your jeans will let you can't know, and besides, it's the last thing on your mind—though it would suck if the bar closed before you finished. At some point you start to think he's grown extra hands but you realize he's sharing you with other men. Your sense of abandonment increases then. Before, you could have said you chose this man, but these other men touching you, using you, having sex with you, these men you didn't choose, nor they you; you have been given to them like a toy. There are hands everywhere now. You are being caressed, fondled, slapped, pinched, prodded, you are being pushed to your knees, things are put in your mouth, hands move your face from crotch to crotch, your mouth on one man, your hands on two others, you are moved from one man to another and then another and you lose the man you had been with and then finally you lose yourself. You are a drill boring into the earth. You are a top spun round and round. You are an umbrella twirling off the drops that fall on it. You are a helicopter whirling into the sky. You are the world, turning on its axis. You are making so many people so happy, but what are you? You know that some people decry this kind of sex for its lack of intimate connection, but how much more connected could you be? You feel lifted and weighted by your attachment with the men touching you. If you knew one more thing about them, if you were to learn even their names, you feel you would explode with excess information. But you remain in a perfect suspended state of contained motion. It's in these pure moments that truth

6. Pain

I believe that the soul exists, but not all the time. It has to be whipped into shape, like an egg cream, like a political party, like a slave. But this calling forth of the soul is fraught, for what is whipped is not the soul but the self. The soul will only come forward when the self is effaced, and afterward, when it has departed, it is the body that must bear the pain of the beating. In your search you find yourself on my bed. I close your eyes and I seal your mouth, I fill your ears and I stuff your nose with amyl, I hide your face from you and from me. On the bed you are a naked body and on the bed you are a body without a head. You are a stranger on my bed, your face and all it signifies hidden from me and your body and all it signifies hidden from you. From now on you can only feel; from now on I can only act. Only I can act and I can only act on the shackled pink X that is your body. The black egg that your head has become retains its mysteries, and inside that egg you are trapped. The distant slapping and lashing and beating and punching are powerless blows against a shell that won't crack, and the pain that you feel, but can't see or hear, or cry out against, or know, or describe, is different from any pain you have ever felt before. Because your external senses have been made useless it moves inside of you, inside your body and then, inevitably, inside your mind, and soon it comes to feel like a part of you. That part of you is a wind, a tornado that lifts you from where you are—my bed, and this world, and your life—and sets you down somewhere else. Later you will be able to say nothing about this place save that whatever is there can't be experienced through the senses, but while you are there you don't even know you're there. Only I know that. When you come back all you know is that you aren't there anymore, and that you hurt. Distant points of violation identify themselves, and the pain you feel in each place is distinct from the pain in each of the other places. For a moment you slip inside each of these pains and for each of these moments you rise a few inches above the bed and are back where you had been. But then you fall, and fall again, again and again you fall until finally a knowledge that is more a yearning than an idea makes you still: you realize that it's only in the moments after it leaves you that you know the soul in terms you can understand, in words, in remembered sensations. That's all. That is all there is, and you know then that you can only lie here bound to the bed at your wrists and ankles but bound to the world by ties even more constraining, and you lie there, and you watch your soul retreat from you, and it retreats from you like the loss of your mother's body.

7. Addiction

Neither the flame shall singe your fingers nor the smoke cloud your lungs. Nor the flame burn your lips, nor the smoke blacken your breath. Nor the flame melt your skin, nor the smoke rot your body. Nor the flame consume the world, nor the smoke wave its banner to the dead. Nor singe, nor burn, nor melt, nor consume; nor cloud, nor blacken, nor rot, nor wave. The only sign, this: the yellow tips of two of your fingers, the mark of habit, of compulsion, of identity, of Cain. Here is your point of departure, here your journey's end. Here is your portable home and here the continuous you. No matter where you are you can look at these yellow tips and locate yourself. Touch them to your lips and you will remember everything you have ever done. Touch them to mine and for that instant I will know you completely.

8. Fear

Then from the horizon black like the wall of a distant cliff comes the wind, washing waves over the bow of the boat and knocking the fire from its place, and then the fire begins to devour the flesh of the boat. Then the men fight the fanned flames with buckets of water and the soil of potted plants and the breath of their lungs and then, suddenly, somehow, the fire is gone. Then for a moment the burned boat rides in the lee of a valley between two high mountains of water, and then the mountains clap together like a pair of hands and the boat is broken apart like matchsticks. Then the men cling to the splinters of their lives and fear a grave in the dark mud far below them and forget forever their voyage of discovery, and they call out in voices drowned by the wind, "We are doomed." And only then does one voice shine forth like a beacon, and in unwavering tones declare, "You are saved."

9. Grief

Coming and Going Blues
for Daniel George Marks, 1957–1988

I been blue all day
I been blue all day
I been thinking 'bout my man
He done come and gone away

He done took up sick
Sick done took up him
Sickness fell down like a storm
Weatherman said It sure looks grim

I watched it take up hold
I watched it take up hold
Wheezing like a tire hit a nail
His skin was hot but now it's cold

Marks showed up on his face

Marks showed up on his face
They showed a map of hurt and pain
I hope he's in a painless place

At the end I took his hand
At the end I took his hand
I said If you wanna leave
Then you know I'll understand

He wasn't here too long
He wasn't here too long
When he was here he was my life
Now he's gone he is my song

I remember our first kiss
Yes, I remember that first kiss
Words fail me to describe it
But that kiss I'm gonna miss

That man was like a castle
And he given me the key
I lived inside his walls
Now he lives inside of me

I'm a-coming home
I'm a-coming home
I'm a-coming home
I'm a-going home

I been blue all day
I been blue all day
Love is gone away, boys
Come and dig my grave

10. Smell

In your bathroom there is a sink, a white oval, the shape of a halved hollowed eggshell, a porcelain bowl that rests upon a porcelain pedestal. Hidden within this pedestal is the pipe that carries away your sink's refuse, which is your refuse: your whiskers and sloughed-off skin cells, hairs that have broken from your head, blood that has leaked from gums or nose or fingers. It is a feature, this sink on its pedestal—so says your landlord—but, in fact, because of the pedestal's narrow width, the pipe within it lacks what plumbers call a trap, that double curve of pipe shaped like an S too lazy to stand upright. The trap is meant to hold water in its valley and so block sewer gases from rising into your bathroom. But your sink lacks this trap: the water from your tap rushes straight back into the earth like rain falling on a windless day, and often, on hot days especially, a fetid smell rises into your house, a thinly but evenly spread stench that takes over your life like the sound of an argument in the house next door. Light a match, your landlord said when you complained, and left it at that. Now, years later, it has become your companion, this stink, something to talk to when you're alone the way other people talk to a pet or to the walls. Oh, it's you again, you say, and you wave a hand, a greeting and a clearing of the air—and, so, a farewell as well. Sometimes, when you awaken in the middle of the night for a pee and there is no smell in your bathroom, you put your face right into the shell of sink and sniff deeply, pulling into your lungs a past that is deeper than memory. Once, after doing this, you stand up and catch sight of yourself in the mirror. Your face spooks you for some reason, and you grab nervously at the book of matches left in a concavity of the sink meant for a bar of soap. You take a match, light it, you hold it to the mouth of the drain. It sputters there, a brief consolation, and then, as if tweaked by fingers, it goes out. Your sleep-glazed eyes stare at a rising ribbon of smoke that seems to offer both rebuke and absolution, and then a second breath, yours or the pipe's, disperses even that illusion, and you are left with nothing but yourself.

11. Death

The hands are the body's conjunctions: they can bring together anything they can grasp, hold, pick up, carry, move, anything they can touch. Look at your hands now, the unmarked left one and the right with its two nicotine-stained fingers. Those hands have touched pens and penises, and food and forks and knives and spoons to eat that food, they have touched your naked body and the clothes that have covered it, and they have touched the hands of living and dying and dead men. They have dug into soft earth and run bunches of freshly mown grass over your skin, tugged daffodils from the ground and pulled your body up the rough trunks of oak trees. They have grasped doorknobs and turned them, and turned back blankets, and turned on taps to release jets of hot and cold water, and they have touched that water. They have run through the grooves in an elephant's skin and untangled the matted mane of a horse and pulled back from the sting of a honeybee. They have held books and tickets and clocks and maps and money and guitars and iron bars, and they have held nothing except air. Oh, how can you stand it, Gordon, how can you bear to think of all your hands have touched, how can you continue to reach out for more? But your soul grows lonely, trapped within its bodily prison, and so there is always that reach for more, for excess, for the fifth cup of coffee, the body in the darkness, the bullet, to slip into the chamber. Dear Gordon, your soul is like the soul of anyone: it reaches out for both good and evil. It is neither good nor evil in itself, for like any creature with two hands you can reach out with your left and touch one thing and reach out with your right and touch another, and your soul reconciles these opposites through the medium of your body. But the search of the soul is really the search *for* the soul, and the search for the soul is, finally, the search for death. One day—one day you will reach out too far to the left and you will reach out too far to the right. You will reach out so far that you will be unable to draw your hands back in, and so you will continue to reach farther and farther out until your body splits open and what is inside is released and shines forth, like a star.

12. Art

What is left is the word: everything else died or departed long ago. What is left is the imagination. If I had to formulate a theory of language then I would say that because our grammar allows us to link any one word with any other— the words "life" and "death," for example, can be joined by a single conjunction—then no word can quite escape all those other meanings. It's not just that nothing is simply one thing, it's that one thing can be, must be everything, and this multiplicity of meanings is, I believe, the writer's only consolation. How else could we live with what little we manage to get on paper? I choose to locate my quest for the soul in you because there is no way something as imprecise as this language can ever arrive at the absolute nature of love, of pain, of hunger, of the soul. There can only be my love, my pain, my hunger, my soul; there can only be your love, your pain, your hunger, your soul; and it's my hope that somewhere in the conjunction between you and me I will arrive at something that is more than either of us. We have, as they say, poured our souls into every word we've written. We've tried with each of those words to communicate a complete vision of the world. We know that art, like radical politics, seeks to make itself unnecessary: embedded somewhere in every poem, every story, every play is a utopian vision that, if achieved, would make the words irrelevant, redundant, unnecessary. You have your vision, I have mine, and I suspect that these visions are closer than we realize; and now I'll reveal something about myself to you: I don't know what good it does to write about someone after they die, but I'm not above thinking that if I write about someone before they die then they'll keep on living. I don't mean that metaphorically, and I don't mean just you. "The epidemic is the revelatory aspect of our time," you wrote in a letter when you were alive, but what it reveals to me and what it revealed to you are not, I think, the same thing. Faced with that, all I can offer is a variation on childhood's dare: I'll show you what AIDS has shown me, if you'll show me what AIDS has shown you.

13. Dreams

Just before I fell asleep I heard water dripping out of the drainpipe in the back garden. Robbie was sleeping beside me; his hand was on my stomach and their steady rise and fall seemed a conjunctive effort. We had just had sex; I was thinking about death. (I am moving away from you Gordon, I know, I am moving back into myself. This is what I meant when I talked about the conjunction of you and me: I am offering a piece of myself to you now, in the hope that you can pick it up and give us both meaning.) The water dripped slowly: the rain had stopped hours ago and what I heard was just the last coalescing drops falling the few inches from the bottom of the pipe to the concrete sidewalk, a slow and surprisingly regular rhythm made more of silence than of splashing. I wondered, then, where the water went, and I thought I remembered the rusted bars of an iron grate, the darkness of a hole visible, or invisible, between its slats. So the water drains from a smaller pipe into a larger, I thought, drop by drop, and then goes where? The canal, I thought, no more than a quarter mile away across

Mile End Park, and as I slid closer to sleep my breathing fell in with Robbie's and my mind fell in with the water, and together—me, the water, and Robbie—squeezed and shimmied our way down that long narrow tunnel until we spilled out into the canal. And the canal carried us to the Thames, and the Thames carried us to the Channel, and the Channel was like the clasped fingers of the Atlantic, holding us in its embrace. I was almost asleep by then, and I thought, children leave their parents this way, and lovers leave each other, and the soul will leave the body like this, like a drop of water making its way back to the ocean, slowly joining and rejoining and joining yet again, until what was whole once becomes, once again, whole.

ALMOST CLOSED

We heated our house in Kansas with a wood-burning stove. Each night the last person still awake had to stoke the fire so it would last till morning. This was a task with which I was finally, occasionally, entrusted in my late teens; it was a clumsy, potentially noisy operation that had to be achieved with some attempt at silence since everyone else was asleep, and I can still feel the weight of the cast-iron shovel in my hands as I tried to skim ash from the stones that covered the stove's bottom without dragging the shovel over their rough surface. The ash had to be removed, the coals consolidated, a few fat logs maneuvered through the stove's narrow door and laid gently atop the glowing pile. I would close the door then, and lean heavily against it so that the metal of its handle wouldn't squeak against the metal of the hasp as I fastened it. Finally, I would adjust the air vent to almost-closed, so that just enough oxygen would enter the stove's interior to keep the flame alive, and then I would go to sleep. Even these precautions weren't enough, and the only way to ensure that the fire would still be going come morning was by checking it during the night. This was the only thing left to chance: no one set an alarm for 3 A.M. or anything, we just hoped someone would wake up. Usually I did. I would lie in the dark for a moment, my body cocooned in blankets, my face exposed and cold; then I would rush to the bathroom and pee; then I would go to the stove and open it quickly, quietly, only a crack. There was something rhapsodic in the moment, something that demanded pause. I stared into the fire, shivering. I looked at the orange embers, tiny, fiercely hot and yet restrained, and only slowly consuming the logs laid on top of them. Air entered the stove and the coals flickered, glowed more brightly; within moments a few flames would have appeared but by then I'd have determined if the fire was okay or if another log was needed, and one way or another the moment passed. The stove and its small warmth were soon resealed, and I returned to my still-warm bed and fell asleep listening to the crackling fire settle into its own version of slumber. In the frigid morning, the stove's vent could be opened wide: in their steel shell the coals would pulse and spit sparks until, with almost concussive suddenness, the logs would burst into flame and heat blaze into the house.

This is one way to live.

(1994)

Visions and Revisions was assembled from more than a dozen different essays written over the course of twenty-five years, many of which were previously published. I want to express my thanks to all the editors who helped me improve these pieces, not least my editor at Soho, Mark Doten, who played an invaluable role in helping me shape this book.